HIS PRESENCE
CHANGES
EVERYTHING

D1306095

HIS PRESENCE CHANGES EVERYTHING

REV. KAREN LEE MOSELY

ISBN 978-0-9840673-6-7
0-9840673-6-1

His Presence Changes Everything

Published by Mountz Media & Publishing
Tulsa, Oklahoma
918.296.0995
www.mountzmedia.com

DEDICATION

I dedicate this book to my wonderful, patient and loving husband, Skip Mosely. You have supported me, accepted me and loved me into the calling of God on our lives. You are the reason we're fulfilling and pursuing God's plan and purpose, and I'm so grateful that we've been honored together by God to stand as one. Thank you for the many sacrifices you have made so we could walk in God's amazing grace and provision for our lives. I love you forever and always.

I also dedicate this book to my precious pastor and friend, Bill McRay, senior pastor of Victory Fellowship Church in Nashville, Tennessee. Where would I be without you and the Holy Spirit in my life? Thank you for all you've sown into my life and calling all these years. It is my honor and blessing to call you father and pastor. Thank you for the patience, acceptance, unconditional love and endless hours of instruction and correction you have sacrificially and lovingly sown into my life. It is with great love and respect I thank you and Pastor Linda. I am eternally grateful to God for giving me the gift of a pastor who introduced me to the truth of God's Word and a life of walking intimately with the Holy Spirit, my best friend. Truly this book would not be a reality without your Holy Spirit relationship, which I saw and caught from following you. I am forever grateful to our Father God for establishing a divine connection, so we may run our race together until Jesus comes.

CONTENTS

CHAPTER 1

CHURCH, RISE UP!

These are the last days. We're living in them now. We're living in a day and a time that God's Word has prophesied would come before the return or Second Coming of Jesus. We're living in a day when the Spirit of God is pouring Himself out upon all flesh as foretold in the book of Acts. Clearly it's no longer yesterday and all that came with days gone by; it's today, and today is the day of the Lord. It's a new season in the realm of the spirit, and it's time for the body of Christ to be empowered, filled and flooded to live and work in the manifest presence of God. God has long been preparing us and getting us ready for this time. He has put everything in us that we would need for this hour and for this day, and the day has arrived.

Naturally speaking, signs of the times surround us and are broadcast in nearly every news headline—wars, rumors of wars, earthquakes, hurricanes, floods and natural disasters of every kind. The earth itself groans as we stand on the horizon of time, and the world grows darker in so many ways. We've come into a time when it's very important that we know the leading of the Lord and we follow the leading of the Lord individually and collectively.

Yet, spiritually speaking, the finest hour of the Church is upon us. The light upon us only grows brighter as the world grows darker. We should expect the world around us to change, and we should expect the Father to change us so we can work in the grace of His outpouring that is on us even now.

From the beginning everything in the Father's heart has been centered around and upon blessing His children. From the beginning He empowered His children to operate in dominion and authority on this earth; that's what God planned and that's what God desires. Unfortunately, as a Church we haven't done very much of that; we haven't explored the depths of dominion and authority given to us. I believe the Church as a whole has walked in only a fraction of what our Father has made available to us. That must change! We must recognize how God is moving in the earth, and we must take hold of His plan and follow Him. Our time has come, for His time has come.

If you're waiting for something to happen or you're waiting for more instruction from heaven before you rise empowered and full of authority, perhaps you need to shift your thinking. Dear friend, recognize that you already have on the inside of you the grace and the power of God to overcome whatever comes along in these uncertain times. No matter what it looks like, no matter how complicated things might appear, no matter what the news headlines proclaim and no matter what transpires in this corridor of time—*you*—have God on the inside of you. Our Father did not leave us as orphans, and He did not leave us helpless; He gave us His Spirit. He gave us *Himself*.

The Prophet Hosea said, "…If we follow on to know the Lord…he shall come unto us as the rain…" (Hosea 6:3 KJV). We often read this verse focusing on the word *rain*, but notice another important phrase. The prophet also said, *"He shall come unto us."* How true! He's coming to us even in this hour, and He's equipping the Church. The rain—or the power, the glory, the blessing—is coming.

Some might say, "Well, I get confused. Are we waiting for the rain to come or the blessing to come or the glory to come?" Don't get confused because it's all the same presence of God. *It's all Him.* It's all good. It's all God, and it's all coming. I'm telling you, the power of God will begin to rise up inside of you; it will rise in you for such a time as this. When it does, it's for you to do something or to say something—it's for you *to be* something.

Rise, Church, and take your place. This Church age is drawing to a close, and there's much work to be done. Your finest hour is at hand.

SHIFTING UPWARD

We are shifting upward, and we must take responsibility now and act like the mature Church we're supposed to be. We're no longer a baby Church, but a Church preparing to be the bride of Christ. There should be a huge and significant difference between the maturity, behavior, skill and ability of a baby and that of an adult bride. So much so that the Holy Spirit is saying to us, "Take responsibility. Take responsibility for your spirit. Take responsibility for your heart. Take responsibility for your tongue. Take responsibility for your life now. Come with Me, and let Me take you places that are ready for you."

Up until this point, some have experienced the manifest glory of God on occasion. But we have not *lived* day by day and moment by moment in the manifest glory or presence of God as a body or a Church. Yet, now we will. Now we *must!* That is what Jesus made available to us through redemption and gave to us—the ability to live in His presence.

It's such an honor and a privilege to experience and partake of the *manifest presence* of God. In fact, the dictionary defines *manifest* as *to make evident or certain by showing or displaying*. In the same way, we can say the manifest presence of God is made evident or certain, shown or displayed to the point that it becomes tangible and manifests in this realm. In other words, the presence of God becomes so real to us that we are tangibly aware of His presence about us in this natural physical world because it is shown forth and evident.

Actually, I've been thinking about how close He really is all the time now, how often His presence manifests in this hour. Earlier we read in Hosea 6:3, "He shall come unto us …," and it's not simply when we get into worship or prayer. I'm sensing and knowing how close He is continually now. *He's moving in on us, and that's why these days must be days of the Holy Spirit.*

We must get to know the Holy Spirit like we've never known Him before because He's the One who knows how to get us where we're going—how to get us to our places in God and how to help us finish our courses. He's the One who must empower and equip us. The Holy Spirit knows how to get His power working in us so He will manifest His glorious presence and power wherever He wants to channel and direct it. You and I are the conductors of the power and anointing of God, and these are the days when the power and anointing will manifest or display itself frequently.

Church, we must be sealed with the presence of God so we're able to follow Him and work with Him. We must expect God to do great and mighty things and expect that He will do them through you and me. We're rising, and we're changing. The Spirit of God is at work in the Church right now bringing change to us. The more light we have, the more darkness that will be uncovered, and the more like Him we become.

Your greatest days are in front of you. Hallelujah! My greatest days are in front of me. Take a minute to say that aloud right now. "My greatest days are in front of me, and I'm shifting upward toward God's highest and best in every area of life."

A TIME OF PREPARATION

The Holy Spirit mentored Jesus all along the way during His earthly ministry, and He's come to mentor the Church for our greatest hour. If you think about it, Jesus prepared and practiced to administer the glory of God for 30 years of His life on earth. Now we must practice, too. Surely that was a long season of preparation for Jesus, and yet it paid off because Jesus changed all humanity and the course of the world in three short years of earthly ministry.

In our case, I don't know how many years we have left before Jesus returns. I don't know if we have one year, two years, three years or more, but I don't think it's a long time. So we might as well get hooked up with His plans and get into place. We must get to know the Holy Spirit and allow Him to work through us. Jesus completely abandoned

WE'RE STANDING ON THE THRESHOLD, ENTERING THE DOORWAY OF A NEW SEASON AND A NEW TIME IN THE REALM OF THE SPIRIT.

and surrendered His own likes and dislikes, and He was completely dependent upon the Holy Spirit to do anything and everything in His life. The Bible tells us that for 30 years Jesus lived by the anointing inside of Him, and that's how He was able to please the Father in all things.

Then when the time came and there was a change for Jesus—when He was on the threshold of the work God destined Him to do—Jesus went across the river Jordan and the windows of heaven opened up. The anointing came upon Him; the Holy Spirit descended upon Him. Jesus was anointed for a new season in His life. His preparation had ended, and His anointed work had begun. This is where we are now, Church. We're standing on the threshold, entering the doorway of a new season and a new time in the realm of the spirit. So we must learn of the anointing and cooperate with it in order to take our places and finish our jobs.

How do we accomplish this? By faith. By faith we must become so fully aware of the anointing that we're dependent on it. We must become very comfortable in the manifest presence of God and learn to walk and to live in this glory of God on a regular basis.

Satan has tried to defeat the Church from rising to its proper place. For the past 10 years he has tried desperately to take the Holy Spirit out of nearly every church he could. I know because I've watched the devil try as I've traveled to minister in churches. Satan has assigned anti-Christ devils and anti-anointing devils for this very task. Yet, when you think about it, it's ridiculous to even try to take the Holy Spirit out of the Church because the Holy Spirit *is* God. That's what my Bible tells me.

That's like saying, "OK, God, we don't need You anymore. We can take it from here." Only Satan is foolish enough to try to talk someone into believing that. The truth is, there never has been and never will be a time in our lives when we can "take it from here." In fact, we're living in a time, a day, an hour when apart from God we can do nothing, and nothing means absolutely nothing.

So, Church, let's allow the Holy Spirit to train us to work in power and glory. Let us lean to Him and look to Him in every facet of our lives. Hallelujah! We're rising, and we're changing.

You're rising, and *you're* changing.

CHAPTER 2

INCREASE COMING

Increase is coming in this day of outpouring, and it's coming on every side. Increase is coming to you, and it's coming for a very definite purpose. The Spirit of God is endeavoring to enlarge us on the inside, so we can receive the fullness of everything God has prepared for us individually and corporately. In other words, the Spirit of God desires to help us make room for more of Himself in our lives.

He must enlarge our capacity to receive because the more we're stretched in Him, the more we can contain of Him. Once we understand that we have the potential to contain all of Him, we should never be satisfied with only a little of Him. We should not be satisfied until He floods our very soul.

You see, at the moment we choose to be born again into the family of God and receive Jesus Christ as our Lord and Savior, we receive a measure of God on the inside of us. The Spirit of God comes to live and dwell on the inside of us (2 Corinthians 6:16). But that's only the beginning. In Acts 2:1-4, the Bible describes a subsequent experience where believers can be endowed and filled with a richer and deeper measure of God through the Baptism of the Holy Spirit.

Yet, there's still more. Being born again and filled with the Spirit are miraculous and marvelous experiences, but there's even more of God available to us, dear friend. Being born again and Spirit filled are the gateway to all things in the spirit realm, where there are never-ending, ever-increasing realms and rooms and places in God to *increase us* from faith to faith and glory to glory.

Let me share with you the definition of the word *increase*. It means *to grow, to come up, to become more violent, to become brighter, to swell, to rise and to enlarge.* These words take on a powerful meaning in the context of the spirit realm. Just when you think you've stretched beyond where you could possibly stretch in the things of the spirit, you can stretch even more.

When you think you've praised God enough, you can stretch to praise Him a little bit more. When you think you've worshipped Him long enough, you can stretch to worship Him a little bit more. When you think you've studied in His Word long enough, you can study a little bit more. When you think you've prayed long enough, you can pray a little bit more.

> ...THERE ARE NEVER-ENDING, EVER-INCREASING REALMS AND ROOMS AND PLACES IN GOD TO INCREASE US FROM FAITH TO FAITH AND GLORY TO GLORY.

Then, in pressing to reach beyond your limitations, you'll stretch your spirit. You'll increase your capacity because you stretched past the place you are comfortable. This determination and effort will stretch and increase your capacity and your hunger for more of Him. And His glory and His presence will come rushing in to fill and satisfy your hunger. His glorious presence will consume the place you have carved out for Him.

Sadly some Christians have spirits about the size of a Dixie cup, and they receive the glory and power of God just enough to fill the ever-so-small cup. After they're full, they cannot contain any more. This principle is true even in the natural realm as it pertains to the amount of food a full stomach can consume and hold. When people are full of food, they're just plain full; that's all they can eat.

Yet, even in the natural, if we eat more, we'll be able to eat more. In other words, if we eat when we're already full, our stomachs increase and stretch. Then our stomachs crave more, and we fill them with more and more. Certainly most of us don't want to increase our physical appetites this way, but nevertheless, this principle works in the natural realm and in the spiritual realm.

Along the same line, we must give out and use what we consume in both the natural and physical realms in order to partake of more. Expending energy in the natural realm increases our bodies' need for more food, more caloric intake, more nutrition. In the same way, giving out of our spiritual resources—serving God and serving people—stretches and enlarges our capacity to receive more of God as well as accessing more of Him inside of us.

The simple but profound truth is that increase in the spirit realm is the key to increase in all other realms. For instance, if we desire to increase in finances, business or relationships, we must first increase in spiritual things. Why? That's how the kingdom of God operates; it operates from within. Religion operates from without; it operates through the seen realm to the unseen realm. But the kingdom of God operates from the unseen realm to the seen realm.

Too often Christians work every natural solution possible here in the natural realm to obtain money, health or the answer to this need or that need. Yet, if the answer we need comes from God, it will come from the spirit realm; it will come from inside and then show up outside. Third John 2 instructs us this way: "Beloved, I pray that you may prosper in all things and be in health, *just as your soul prospers*" (NKJV). Therefore, in order for us to increase in our natural lives, we must first increase in our spiritual lives.

FAITH: THE ROAD TO INCREASE

Most of us recognize that the Spirit of God is everywhere all the time, around us all the time and always and forever inside every born again believer. But we must also recognize that the leading and the presence of the Holy Spirit can be crowded out by this seen realm where we live and see and feel.

In other words, our five senses crowd out the presence of God in our lives and alter our focus. Therein lies a problem because the Christian life is not supposed to be a life led by the senses or by what we see, feel, hear, think or touch. Rather, the Christian life is supposed to be lived out of our spirits through faith.

I've observed in my life and in the lives of others, that too often we reach a point where we only use our faith in times of trouble. For instance, we use our faith when we need finances; we use our faith when we need healing; we use our faith when we need help in relationships. When we *need something* from God, *then* we begin using faith. We live from crisis to crisis.

But that is not how we're instructed to live according to the Word of God. Romans 1:17 says *the just* should *live* by faith. Who are *the just?* We are. We are God's people, and we are the just. God made us just or righteous by the blood of Jesus, and our instruction is to *live by faith*. Do you understand what this requires? God's plan is not that we pull faith out of storage to use when we're in trouble. No, God's plan is that we live all day—every single day—by faith. It's not a single step, but a continual walk because God desires that we live a *lifestyle of faith.*

Christians who live by faith can live from increase to increase and glory to glory—living the life God gave us. Earthly living is living from crisis to crisis, but Jesus came to give us a higher life. Jesus intends for us to live *His life* on earth.

Actually, this is why some Christians get bored with God, with the Word, with church, with life and with everything. Why? Because they're not living life the way God meant it to be, and they're not exercising their faith for the life of adventure, abundance, joy and prosperity spirit, soul and body that God planned.

Take note. No matter how it has been in the past, in this day and hour of the Church, we *must* live by the spirit of faith. In fact, plain and simple, that's what gives us success in this life. The body of Christ has been taught faith for years now, so the deposits God has made in us can now draw out a spirit of faith.

What is a spirit of faith? It's a strong, pioneer spirit that will enable you to overcome and possess the land. A spirit of faith always possesses the land and takes back everything the enemy has tried to steal. Faith won't be denied. The spirit of faith stands boldly in the face of opposition and says, "That's mine, and you better move on. I'm taking the land. I'm taking healing. I'm taking deliverance. I'm taking blessing. I'm taking the goodness of God." A spirit of faith is absolutely unstoppable. A spirit of faith won't be pushed back, but instead pushes back every enemy of its faith.

Even more, a spirit of faith irritates and agitates the spirit of doubt. The spirit of doubt wants to complain, murmur and question why things don't change and why they haven't changed. Yet, friend, complaining and murmuring is dangerous to your spirit because it connects you to the spirit of doubt. It extinguishes your faith. You can only access God by faith, so consequently you can receive nothing of Him without it. The God kind of faith is the only way we can access the spirit realm, where everything you need is provided.

NO CONDEMNATION ALLOWED

You absolutely will never hear the Holy Spirit talk anything but faith. He doesn't murmur ever, and He complains never. He has nothing to say about anything except a good report. That's who He is. He *is* the Good Report, and that's what He always has to say. You and I should be the same way, following His example and refusing to talk anything but faith.

Nevertheless, no matter how hard we work to do right and talk right and live by faith, we still will have occasion to make a mistake or miss it now and then. When those times occur, know that there's help available. We have only but to ask for forgiveness, and the power of Jesus' blood will cleanse us completely.

I recall a time I missed it for sure. After a service where I had ministered, we went out to enjoy fellowship with a few people. When I returned to my hotel room, I became really convicted by the Holy Spirit about some matters that were discussed. The Holy Spirit even spoke to me, saying, "I wouldn't have said that; I wouldn't have talked like that."

Nevertheless, I'm here to tell you that when the Holy Spirit convicts us, He doesn't condemn us. He never condemns because condemnation makes us feel as if we're incapable of succeeding in life. It piles negativity on top of negativity, and that's certainly not the Holy Spirit. Actually, guilt can be cruel. That's why there's simply no place for condemnation in the walk of faith. Thank You, Jesus, for Your blood that cleanses us. You are so sweet, and You are for us. You are our deliverance and our way out.

In my situation, I repented, and my Father forgave me. The Bible says godly sorrow leads to repentance, and it does. I grieved Him, and I knew in my heart I had sinned against Him.

But when I repented and asked for forgiveness, I knew just as quickly that He had forgiven me because 1 John 1:9 says, "If we confess our sins, He is faithful and just to forgive us our sins and to cleanse us from all unrighteousness" (NKJV). I knew I was forgiven because He promised me in His Word that He would. I didn't have to base my confidence on a feeling. It's so important to *know* that you're forgiven because if you wait until you *feel forgiven*, you could wait a long time.

Of course, you realize that instead of repenting what your flesh really wants to do is to somehow get out of the situation altogether. It wants to say, "Well now, God, You know I didn't really mean to say that or do that thing." Yes, that's the flesh. The flesh is all about making excuses, but excuses don't work with God; He doesn't even hear them. He's righteous and just, and He forgives. He also called us to repent and not make excuses or blame others for our sins. Jesus is our justification and freedom from self-justification.

Still, our flesh likes to try to justify itself and say things like, "Now, God, You know my heart." Well, yes, God does know our hearts, and He declared, "Keep your heart with all diligence, For out of it spring the issues of life" (Proverbs 4:23 NKJV). He declared that "...out of the abundance of the heart the mouth speaks" (Matthew 12:34 NKJV). Hmmm, those excuses evaporated into thin air. So when we said He should know what is in our hearts, He surely does because we spoke out exactly what was in our hearts. The truth is, we simply don't have excuses, but we do have the blood of Jesus. Hallelujah!

Here's what I've learned: Don't even bother to give God excuses. Forget that whole notion because it doesn't work. Instead, when we do wrong, we simply need to put our mistake under Jesus' blood, receive the mercy the blood provides us and move on from there. We all make mistakes. We all miss it, and that's why God gave us simple instructions to reconcile us back to Him. The Bible instructs us to confess to our Father, and He will be faithful and just to forgive us. It's a marvelous provision His love has gifted to us.

So let me encourage you to go directly to Him when you miss it and tell Him, "Father, I confess such and such to You, and I put it under the blood. I ask You to forgive me, and I thank You that You forgive me and cleanse me of that unrighteousness. Dear Father, cleanse my heart, cleanse my mind and cleanse my soul. I apply the blood over my heart, mind and soul, and I receive Your forgiveness."

Then, when you receive forgiveness, condemnation and guilt are all removed. Notice that God's Word says so. Romans 8:1 says, "Therefore, [there is] now no condemnation (no adjudging guilty of wrong) for those who are in Christ Jesus, who live [and] walk not after the dictates of the flesh, but after the dictates of the Spirit."

Oh the glory of that! When you've asked and received forgiveness, your Father doesn't remember the transgression any longer (Hebrews 10:17). If you brought it back to Him, He would say, "I don't know what you're talking about. All is under the blood." Hallelujah! If it's under the blood, then it's gone. "As far as the east is from the west, So far has He removed our transgressions from us," Psalm 103:12 (NKJV) says. He remembers it no more; it's gone in the blood. It's forgiven, forgotten and forever removed.

Now symptoms of unrighteousness may try to attach themselves to your feelings and say, "You're so unworthy. You just don't deserve anything. You'll never get it together in your life. You simply cannot make the mark." Actually, that's exactly what I began thinking after speaking things that grieved the Holy Spirit while fellowshipping with people after church. I speak from experience.

Quite honestly, I was so unforgiving toward my own

behavior that it began to affect my ministry. That next morning I said out loud, "God, I cannot go preach. I just cannot go out there and preach."

But I'll never forget how the Spirit of God answered me. He said, "You know, when you did that is not when I found out about it. That's when you found out about it. Now you pick yourself up, and you put yourself back over in the righteousness of My Son. You hold your head up and get up and go do what I tell you to do."

Praise Him, that's the way God is, and that's the way the Holy Spirit is. You'll have to shake off those feelings of unrighteousness and unworthiness. You'll have to shake off those feelings of "I'm no good and things never work out for me." All those feelings amount to nothing but doubt and unbelief, so put a stop to them in your life. The righteousness and worth God has given you is a truth, but you cannot receive it through a feeling. You receive it because God said it, and you take Him at His Word. Therefore, He said it and you become it because you believe Him.

Did God not call all of us to walk by faith? Of course, He did. And along the pathway of faith, we cannot let anything or anyone—including ourselves—deter us from living a life of faith.

CHAPTER 3

A GENERAL'S EXAMPLE

God is calling every one of us nearer and nearer to Him in these last days. He's not calling us nearer in physical distance, but nearer to Himself so we can experience more of His presence in our lives. He longs to impart deeper and richer measures of Himself to us.

God has realms of glory and realms of His manifest presence awaiting each of us that are almost more magnificent and exhilarating than we can fathom. He expects us to be walking, talking displays of His glory and His presence. Even now He is summoning us closer, and that's why I want to share some things out of my heart about where we're called to go in Him.

CARRYING GOD'S GLORY

When I think of someone displaying God's glory, one of our great generals and saints in the body of Christ particularly comes to mind. Rev. Vicki Jamison-Peterson carried the presence of God everywhere she went all of the time and amazingly so. She went home to heaven to be with the Lord in 2008, and there's a part of me that misses her greatly. Vicki was a dear friend to me in many ways and a mentor in my life. In fact, observing her life caused me to see and know that the presence of God was not something we could only experience on rare occasions, but that it could become our way of life.

Actually, as I meditated on sharing some of the lessons the Holy Spirit taught me through Vicki's life, I also considered other anointed generals and marvelous leaders in God's army who also taught me valuable lessons. But I believe that sharing about Vicki's life helps me best articulate a life lived in the presence of God because that was Vicki's passionate pursuit through life. She desired to experience the manifest presence of God at all times in all places. And so she did. Vicki lived her life in the glory.

Actually, that same presence of God on her life was manifested in her memorial service as well. I don't think I've ever been in a home-going service quite like hers, where the anointing that rested on the person's life was actually present in that person's memorial service as well. But the glory of God and the presence of God on Vicki's life were ever so present in her memorial service. It many ways it was not a great surprise because Vicki loved the glory of God and carried it always.

I'm so happy for her. She finally got out of her body, which she had desired for a long time. She so desired to step over to the other side in glory—to be present with her Lord—because she knew the other side better than she knew this side. Even while she was here on earth, in many ways she lived on that other side. In the words of the old hymn, she was truly a person for whom the things of this world had grown strangely dim because she knew how to live in those glory places in God.

The presence of God flowed through her and was ever

present in her meetings, but the manifest presence of God also surrounded her personally. It was so evident to those of us around her, and I can truly say that when you were around Vicki, you would start thinking about Jesus. I can explain it best by saying Vicki was a woman dead to this world, but alive into God.

So as I sat in her memorial service, I found myself sitting in the anointing she carried upon her life while she was on earth. It was amazing to sit there and be saturated in the presence of God all the while celebrating Vicki's home going. The tears being shed throughout the room were not because she had left this earth, but because the presence of God filled that place and charged the atmosphere.

You could feel the presence of God in that room just as you could feel the presence of God when you were around her. It was just so Vicki to live in an environment of God's presence. The service had quite an impact on me, and it started me thinking and reflecting so much so that it caused me to move forward in a new and different way.

ABUNDANT ENTRANCE

In many ways, Vicki's departure impacted us all. When a person like Vicki Jamison-Peterson, who carried a significant mantle of anointing, leaves the earth that departure accesses an *abundant entrance* into heaven, and we're all affected.

Let me explain. When a saint of God with an anointing of magnitude departs the earth, the mantle on him or her creates an abundant entrance or an opening into the heavenlies, and therefore, also a wide opening into the earth. In other words, the mantle upon him or her creates an access in the heavenlies to open and bring forth what is stored up for the earth.

I'm telling you when Vicki ascended into the heavenlies, there was an abundant entrance and a wide place of glory opened to the Church as a whole. Glory! And what are these days that we walk in now? *Days of glory.* Yes! Vicki's departure opened a wide place so things that had been stored up for the earth for these end times were able to come through to the earth.

Let's look at scriptures that explain this principle. The Bible tells us that there always has been an access of heaven and earth. There always has been a connection between the two because God connected heaven and earth together. Remember in Genesis 28 where Jacob dreamed of the ladder? Verse 12 says, "Then he [Jacob] dreamed, and behold, a ladder was set up on the earth, and its top reached to heaven; and there the angels of God were *ascending and descending* on it" (NKJV).

Angels were ascending and descending unto heaven and ascending and descending all the time. This is God's plan that the whole earth be filled with the glory of God; it's God's plan that heaven fill the earth with the glory that is in heaven.

Let me give you a few more Bible examples. When Jesus left the earth, He made an abundant entrance into the heavenlies. There was a wide opening created by the anointing upon Him, and as a result the Holy Spirit was poured out upon the 120 people who were waiting in the Upper Room. Because the 120 were in a place of prayer, they accessed what was stored up for the earth. So we could say when Jesus made an abundant entrance into heaven, it brought something down to earth. Or rather, something going up brought something down.

In Isaiah 6 we read how when King Uzziah died, the prophet Isaiah saw the Lord high and lifted up. A place had opened in the heavenlies that enabled Isaiah to see the Lord. In Acts 7:55-56 we read how Stephen died and the heavens were opened and the glory and light of heaven were seen. Then a few chapters later in Acts 9:3-5 we read how light opened Saul's eyes to see here on earth.

You may think, *But when the bright light shined around Saul on the road to Damascus, he was actually blinded.* Naturally speaking, it is a fact that

Saul was blinded by the light from heaven, but spiritually speaking he could see for the first time. In other words, he lost sight of the world so he could gain sight of heaven.

Again, when anointing ascends more can descend. That's how ascending and descending unto God works. *That's why every time you go to the throne of God in prayer, you access something in God that in turn opens up something in you. That's why prayer is so vital in your life.*

Actually, the very first time I heard the phrase *abundant entrance* it was spoken by 20th century prayer warrior Phil Halverson. At that time nobody knew very much about abundant entrance, but he would pray those words often as saints would depart the earth and go home to heaven. People around him didn't understand or recognize what he was doing, but this great man of prayer even prayed out his own home going. Can you imagine? "Abundant entrance, abundant entrance," he used to pray, and, oh, the voice of that man. "Abundant entrance, home, home," and he prayed himself on home to heaven.

But, again, Vicki's departure to heaven opened a wide place of glory to the Church because of the glory on her life. The amazing thing about Vicki Jamison-Peterson was that she walked in the manifest presence of God all the time. Vicki did not simply tap in to the presence of God before services where she would minister or in times of deep prayer. I watched her access the presence of God at all times so much so that it became her lifestyle.

If Vicki was at home with just a few people, she was accessing His presence. If she walked into a restaurant, she was accessing His presence. I walked into a restaurant with Vicki one time to eat lunch, and she immediately walked over to a woman who obviously appeared not to feel well. Vicki wasn't spooky or super spiritual or anything of the kind, but she grabbed the woman's arm and said, "How are you doing today?"

Knowing Vicki as I did and having learned from being around her, I recognized that she was accessing the presence of

God. It might have appeared as though Vicki simply stood there conversing with the woman who was experiencing symptoms, but I watched her the entire

time and knew she was releasing anointing into the women's body as she held onto her arm. Vicki didn't go up and say, "Bam, you're healed!" No, she simply walked with God and imparted His anointing to someone in need.

Dear Church, this is our calling in this hour. This is what we all have available to us. We are invited, called and summoned to walk in the glory of Him.

We must become a people who walk with God and who access the manifest presence of God in our lives daily in all circumstances—moment by moment no matter where we are or what we're doing. Unlimited realms of God's presence await us.

KEENLY AWARE OF GOD

I'm so thankful to God that He has granted me the opportunity through the years to learn from my own fellowship with the Holy Spirit and from others He placed in my life such as Vicki and the late Brother Kenneth E. Hagin, a prophet and teacher who stepped over to glory in 2003. They were people who walked in a deep intimate relationship and fellowship with God. Another person very influential in my spirit walk is my pastor of many years, Bill McRay, who also walks in a deeply intimate relationship and fellowship with God. He so impacted my life in God and mentored me for many years in the Word and the ways of the Holy Spirit.

The one important key I've observed from their lives and relationships with God is that they all have been *keenly aware that God was in them, the hope of glory.* It may sound simple, yet it's so profound.

In the same way, if you desire to walk in the presence of God, you must keep yourself very aware of "...Christ in you, the hope of glory" (Colossians 1:27 NKJV). You and I must be ever aware that Christ dwells in us. Each of us must be ever saying and recognizing: "It's Christ in me, the hope of glory. It's Jesus in me, the hope of glory. Within me dwells Jesus Christ. Within me dwells the anointed One and His anointing. And it is His life in me now that I live by every day."

You see, as a result of the curse that fell on mankind in the Garden of Eden, man and woman became more aware of this physical world that we contact with our natural senses. From the beginning God planned that Adam and Eve walk in fellowship with Him as their spirits dominated them. It was God's plan that Adam and Eve enjoy continual fellowship with Him in the Garden and rule in authority over the earth through their oneness with God.

But when Adam and Eve sinned and fell from grace, sin entered the earth and a curse fell on mankind. That changed everything, but God immediately set about resolving the situation, and that's why God sent Jesus to redeem us from sin. Praise God! Through Jesus' death, burial and resurrection, we are now restored to fellowship with our Father. Jesus destroyed the works of the devil and offered every single man and woman restoration to the Father. Once again we can walk in unbridled fellowship with the Father. Once again we can walk in health and wisdom and blessing as the Father originally planned. Hallelujah! What a good God He is.

However, as long as we're in these bodies of flesh and blood, we will still have to daily rule over our flesh and its natural earthly desires. We still must silence the flesh in all its carnal ways to allow our spirits to rule and dominate in our everyday lives.

In order to contact the spiritual realm, we must use our spiritual senses; it's the only way to communicate with God. Why? Because God is a spirit and we also are spirits. Look with me at two important scriptures on this topic. John 4:24 says, "God is a Spirit: and they that worship him must worship him in spirit and in truth" (KJV). So to fellowship with God, we must communicate in spirit and in truth.

Then notice 1 Thessalonians 5:23 that identifies our three-part make up, "Now may the God of peace Himself sanctify you completely; and may your whole *spirit, soul, and body* be preserved blameless at the coming of our Lord Jesus Christ" (NKJV). In other words, you are a spirit, you have a soul and you live in a body of flesh.

Your spirit is the *real you*, or the "hidden man of the heart" as 1 Peter 3:4 (KJV) says. Your spirit is that part of you that becomes born again and communicates with God. The Bible tells us that your soul is a combination of your mind, will and emotions, and of course, your body is the flesh that covers you like a coat. Amazingly enough, your spirit "man" or inward person of the heart has spiritual eyes and spiritual ears and is a whole spiritual being inside of you.

Even more to the point here, there is a spiritual touch of God that can come upon you, and when it comes upon you, it will mark you. That's what I loved about Vicki; when she opened her mouth, she spoke words from heaven. She knew how to have a good time, but her words were weighty; they were a punch, and they marked you. It was so because she walked with God here on earth.

Vicki didn't walk in and out of faith. She was not walking in doubt and unbelief 20 days of the month, but walking in faith the other 10 days or so. Vicki didn't lay aside the things of the

Spirit for days and days and then spring up saying, "Oh, oh, oh, now I have to hurry and get in faith because there's a lot going on now. Oh, trouble has raised its ugly head. Oh, I have symptoms. Oh, I need finances. Oh, I need direction. Oh, where's my Bible? Oh, oh, oh, I better get prayed up now."

No, Vicki just kept walking and walking and walking with God day in and day out. She was more aware of Him in her than she was aware of who she was in the flesh or her natural body, and it showed. It defined her life and her relationship with God. It marked her.

Actually, it's Satan who works hard to make you more aware of your flesh than your spirit. Satan works hard to make you more aware of your mental and physical and emotional needs and responses. He strives to get you to live your life with everything all about you, surrounded and involved and focused on what makes you happy and what makes you feel good.

He wants you to live your whole life dictated by the desires of the flesh. That's his technique right there. By making you more aware of your flesh, he keeps you out of the spirit. Obviously Satan understands what some Christians do not. He understands that if we sow to the spirit, we reap life; if we sow to the flesh, we reap destruction.

The devil knows very well that if you make contact with the Spirit of God, your answers will come. Your healing will come. Your deliverance will come. Your hope and your blessing will come, and everything you will ever need will flow out of that spiritual relationship and connection with your heavenly Father.

So, the devil tries to steal our God-inheritance by keeping us more aware of the flesh. He also understands that the more aware we are of our own flesh, the more aware we become of other people's flesh. Then we just plain get in the flesh with people or we live according to the appetites of the flesh instead of the fruit of the Spirit. That opens the door to a world of hurt and rejection and sin and temptation. It opens the door to every evil thing the devil throws at us to defeat us. That's how he works it, and it's not very complicated.

Yet, Vicki was an example of a Christian who learned to live her life very aware of God; she lived her life in the presence of God. I watched Vicki live her life that way, and it provided an example for us all.

Did you ever attend one of her meetings? If you did, I know you sensed the tangible presence of God that marked her meetings. However, the tangible presence of God wasn't *only* in her meetings. It was the same if you enjoyed lunch with Vicki or visited her home. She was very aware of God at all times, and so God's presence simply hung around Vicki wherever she was and whatever she was doing. I learned what was available to me by watching her live in God's presence. And that's why I'm sharing about her life with you, so you also can learn what's available in the presence of God.

A HEART CONNECTION

The first time I came in contact with Vicki she was conducting a revival in Alabama. Lucy McKee, a woman of great prayer who has since gone home to be with Lord, had become the assistant pastor of a church in Alabama and began praying for revival and for the glory of God in her church. Truly, the whole area where the church was located became saturated with the presence of God. Through their prayers, the presence of God touched a military base there, and miracles happened left and right.

Meanwhile, in 1994 I had begun my own ministry after being sent out by the local church where my husband, Skip, and I had served our pastor for 15 years. Another minister and I attended that prayer conference together, and the glory of God was so strong. Vicki was often on the platform praying.

After the meetings we were invited to Vicki's home. From the first minute we walked in, we realized that though the church meeting had drawn to a close, God was not at all finished. He was still definitely among us. Actually, God lived in manifestation in Vicki's house. I remember crying as I walked in the front door because the presence of God was so strong in that place. Some people laugh and some people cry when they encounter the presence of God, and sometimes it's all different, but I began to cry that night as I sensed God so strongly in her home.

I'm telling you, Church, this is the answer we need in this day. We need the manifest presence of God permeating our nations, our cities, our churches, our homes, our lives. There is a dimension of God you'll never know otherwise because we know God by knowing His Spirit and His Word and by experiencing His presence. There's a part of God that you'll never know in life unless you experience His manifest presence and bask in it and learn to live in it.

Once you've tasted His presence, a deep hunger for more will continue growing in you. In some ways it's like an addiction because once you've experienced it, you simply cannot live without it. David described it well when he said to the Lord, "...A day in Your courts is better than a thousand [anywhere else]..." (Psalm 84:10).

At Vicki's home that evening after the meetings, we simply fellowshipped together and everyone talked of God. It was a place full of God. As I prepared to leave, Vicki grabbed hold of my arm and gazed directly in my eyes. We had never met before, but she said some things to me about my ministry that just nailed me completely; her words hit the punch and hit the mark. Actually, she exhorted me and corrected me in some areas and said, "If you don't get this right, you're going to cause some situations and challenges for your body." One of the things she said was, "You're busy and going way too much; you're not pacing yourself rightly."

"Don't do that!" she said. "I made that mistake, and my body has suffered greatly because of it. Don't destroy your body!" She said some other things, and truly I was marked, and so was the minister who was with me. We got in the car and our mouths dropped open.

"She nailed you," my friend said.

"Yes, she did," I responded. "She really did." So from that time on there was just this sweet connection between Vicki and me.

DAILY AWARENESS OF GOD

There's no question that Vicki lived her life keenly aware of the manifest presence of God. Yet, consider this, dear friend. We also—everyone who bears the name Christian—are called to live the same way. We are called and invited to live our lives keenly and daily aware of the presence of God because this is how Jesus walked.

There were men in the Old Covenant who walked with God, and this is how men of the new covenant are empowered to walk. The only difference between the two is that men and women of the new covenant have the Spirit of God deposited inside of them. That means the Spirit of God is inside *you*. Jesus life is in *you*.

Let me encourage you to be faithful and diligent to continue developing an awareness of God every day.

The more you develop the awareness of who is in you, the less you'll be aware of who you are without and apart from Him.

It will change life as you know it.

As you develop a deeper awareness of God, it will create a deeper measure of relationship and fellowship with the all-glorious Father. It will drive out defeat from your life as you become so supremely aware and conscious of the greater— much greater—One in you. "...Greater is He that is in you..."

(1 John 4:4 KJV) will no longer be simply a scripture you quote, but much, much more. It will become your experience. It will be a declaration that you are accessing and cultivating the presence of God, and it will begin defining who you are.

CHAPTER 4

ACCESSING GOD'S GLORY

As you become more and more keenly aware of God's presence inside you, you'll begin to know that within you is everything you need or could ever possibly need. You'll begin to know that within you is the righteousness of God. Within you is the wisdom of God. Within you is the direction of God. Within you is the healing of God. Within you is the deliverance of God, and within you is the prosperity and blessing of God.

All of these things and many more are in *you* because the all-knowing, almighty Creator of the universe has deposited them in you. First John 2:27 says He has put His anointing in you, which means He has put *Himself* in you. It's vitally important that you identify the location of His presence because it's in *you*. Yes, all the realms of God have been deposited inside of you—inside of every born again believer. Truly the answer to every need in every situation awaits on the inside of you.

For a certainty, at any moment of need all you must do is access the glory—the power or presence of God on the inside of you—because God has downloaded it there with your supernatural supply.

You cannot access all the blessings of God out here in this natural, physical realm where you see, feel, hear and contact things around you with your five natural senses. If you're looking outward for answers—out here in the natural, physical realm—then you're looking in the wrong place. As we've discussed before, God is a spirit, and you are a spirit, so you will receive from Him out of the realm of the spirit. You will receive from the Spirit who indwells you.

> . . . AT ANY MOMENT OF NEED ALL YOU MUST DO IS ACCESS THE GLORY—THE POWER OR PRESENCE OF GOD ON THE INSIDE OF YOU—BECAUSE GOD HAS DOWNLOADED IT THERE WITH YOUR SUPERNATURAL SUPPLY.

Glory to God, the multifaceted anointing of God is in *you*, and by faith you can draw upon the anointing—the glory, the presence, the power—inside you *any time you want*. In fact, do you realize that *you* decide how much anointing you access?

The choice is completely yours.

You can access only a little bit of anointing or you can access the full anointing of Jesus Himself inside you.

In Ezekiel 47:1-12 we read about a vision God gave the prophet Ezekiel describing measures of water that symbolize levels of anointing available in the life of a Christian. Ezekiel described how an angel measured out water that was ankle deep. Another measure of water came up to the knees and another to the loins. Then there was yet another measure of water where it was high enough to swim.

How much anointing do you want to step into and access for your life? It is my prayer that you will continually access the glory and cultivate His presence. When you come up on a situation and need wisdom, begin to say, "Father, I'm reaching to the wisdom of God inside me. I'm drawing on the Spirit of You in me, and I thank You, Father. I thank You that the wisdom of God is in me because You're in me."

Everything that belongs to you—your entire spiritual heritage—is awaiting you in the realm of the spirit. It's all there. Healing is in you. Deliverance is in you. Wisdom is in you. Prosperity is in you. You only need to reach inside by faith and connect with the anointing, and then by the anointing of God you will prosper. Purpose to pray like this: "I prosper by the anointing of God. I have wisdom, and I know what to do. I'm making right decisions, and the counsel of God is guiding me. The Spirit of God is leading me."

ACKNOWLEDGE HIM TO CONNECT

Let me share with you how the Holy Spirit taught me years ago to develop and build fellowship and relationship with Him. I believe it will do the same for you and help you access His power and presence in your life.

First of all, the Holy Spirit encouraged me to read chapters 14-16 in the Gospel of John, which describe the ministry of the Holy Spirit. Of course, Jesus has instructed all of us to read these chapters and every other Bible chapter and for good reason. Yet, before Jesus returned to heaven after His earthly ministry, Jesus said, "I'm going to leave, but first I want to tell you something that will help you."

Actually, I read these chapters often and encourage you to do the same. As I've meditated on them, I've considered that Jesus' disciples must surely have wondered how it could possibly be better for Jesus not to remain with them on earth.

Yet, Jesus Himself introduced the person of the Holy Spirit by explaining to them and to us in John 16:7, "…I am telling you nothing but the truth when I say it is profitable (good, expedient, advantageous) for you that I go away. Because if I do not go away, the Comforter (Counselor, Helper, Advocate, Intercessor, Strengthener, Standby) will not come to you…but if I go away, I will send Him to you [to be in close fellowship with you]."

We realize the magnitude and significance of what Jesus imparted to us as we read John 16:13-14, which says, "But when He, the Spirit of Truth (the Truth-giving Spirit) comes, He will guide you into all the Truth (the whole, full Truth). For He will not speak His own message [on His own authority]; but He will tell whatever He hears [from the Father; He will give the message that has been given to Him], and He will announce and declare to you the things that are to come [that will happen in the future]. He will honor and glorify Me, because He will take of (receive, draw upon) what is Mine and will reveal (declare, disclose, transmit) it to you."

Jesus explained in these chapters that He was sending the Holy Spirit who would come to live inside every born-again Christian to lead, help, teach and show us things to come. The Comforter, Counselor, Helper, Advocate, Intercessor, Strengthener and Standby would not simply be with us, but live inside us. How magnificent that the very same Holy Spirit that lived in Jesus can live in you and me. Glory!

Jesus knew how vital the Holy Spirit's role would be in our lives, and that's why Jesus revealed the person of the Holy Spirit to us in these chapters. Jesus even made a point of saying in John 16:13 that the Holy Spirit speaks to us what He hears the Father say.

But let me emphasize something important to you. Jesus wasn't talking about you knowing or recognizing the Holy Spirit and His leading in your mind, your head or your brain. No, He wasn't talking about the mental realm at all. It's critical that you understand that all communication with the Holy Spirit must be conducted spirit to spirit by faith. Therefore, to know anything from the Holy Spirit—to be lead, taught, directed or shown anything—you must draw from your spirit by faith.

Every transaction with heaven must be conducted by the spirit by faith.

It's all about faith—by faith, by faith, by faith—and by faith. You can *only know and receive* from God by faith; it's the only way.

By faith you access the anointing of wisdom on the inside of you. By faith you access every kind of anointing of God on the inside of you. So begin to say, "Holy Spirit, You always show me things to come. You are the revealer of Jesus to me. You are the voice that I know."

That's right—*you do know Him!*

How can I be so sure? Jesus Himself said, "You know Him" in John 14:7. Jesus gave you His Word on it.

Then notice the words Jesus spoke in John 10 when He described Himself as a shepherd and those who follow Him as His sheep. Jesus said, "…The sheep follow him, [their shepherd, and Jesus is our Shepherd] for they know his voice. Yet they will by no means follow a stranger, but will flee from him, for they do not know the voice of strangers" (verses 4-6 NKJV).

Isn't that good news, dear friend? You know Him, and you know His voice because Jesus said you do. Jesus said He's the voice of your good Shepherd and another voice you will not follow. So how do you not follow the voice of another? *By faith.* Begin to say, "By faith I never follow the voice of another; I only follow the voice of my good Shepherd."

The Holy Spirit taught me that every time we speak aloud phrases such as these, we connect ourselves more and more with the anointing and the wisdom already on the inside of us. As you open your mouth to say, "I follow the Spirit of God. I know the Spirit of God. I hear from Him. I never follow the voice of another," you are acknowledging the Holy Spirit in your life. You are acknowledging Him and thereby connecting with Him—His Person and His ministry—and you're connecting to supernatural help in whatever area it's needed. Your faith is in action.

Again, let me encourage you with this most important point: Through the words of your mouth, you acknowledge and connect to the Spirit of God. As you speak these truths, you are *connecting* more and more to the voice of the Holy Spirit rather than the voice of your flesh.

Your flesh most certainly also has a voice, and quite frankly, this is where every Christian's biggest problem is—the flesh. You know what the flesh wants to do? It wants to do very little. Actually, the flesh is very lazy. Here's what it usually has to say, "You've done enough. You don't need to do any more." It says, "Nobody appreciates you. Nobody notices what you've done. Nobody even knows you're around." Sound familiar? That's not all—oh no, the flesh has a lot to say. It tries to convince you to give up and quit. It says, "Just sit down! Give up! What's the use? You deserve a break today. You deserve to sit on that couch and watch TV. You deserve to rest, so give yourself a break."

> THROUGH THE WORDS OF YOUR MOUTH, YOU ACKNOWLEDGE AND CONNECT TO THE SPIRIT OF GOD.

Of course there is a place where you should and must give yourself a physical rest because you can violate the laws of caring for your body, and that's the truth. But overall, there's way too much rest in the body of Christ. The flesh is defeating us, Church. Yes, that's right. *The devil isn't defeating us, the flesh is defeating us by making us spiritually complacent and spiritually apathetic and spiritually lazy.*

"Ohhh," the flesh says, "I don't want to pray today. I don't feel like it today so I won't." And off we go—and along with us go the help and the anointing we so desperately need.

Dear Church, hear this truth, and it will change your life: *Everything you need is already right inside you. Truly, His presence changes everything!*

Let these words soak in because they carry revelation and truth. This very principle explains and answers why many Christians have been defeated and why some seem to wait and wait and wait for things to happen in their lives.

Bless their hearts, some Christians will travel to every church they can find looking for someone to pray for them. Of course God anoints people with special graces to pray for us, and yet, someone else praying for us is not always necessary because every born again Christian has God on the inside to meet every possible need or want.

The answer to every question, the direction for every decision, the healing for every body and the provision for every need—is as close as the very air we breathe. Where's your help? GOD is your help. And He's *right inside of you.* Locate Him in you today. He *is* there.

CHAPTER 5

DAILY SUPPLY AND PORTION

Every day you are loaded with new blessings as you communicate and connect with heaven. Every day there is a level in God that He wants for you. In fact, every single day the Spirit of God has a level for you to come up to, and that level that you arise to meet is His supernatural supply for whatever you will encounter that day. As you allow Him to bring you up to that daily portion, He's able to meet every need you have, and that is how each day is sufficient unto itself.

You see, your Father knows your future better than you know your past, and He knows how to meet your needs. God knows the level of light and the level of truth that will meet and surpass whatever occurs and comes into your life on a given day. If you will only free Him and access His presence and power on the inside of you, you'll overcome and triumph over every challenge that comes your way. It won't be a theory or a formula of how you could live victoriously, but it will be your daily experience. It will be your continual testimony.

ALWAYS WITH YOU

In John 14 Jesus said the Holy Spirit is always with you—
always. Actually, however, the Holy Spirit is a whole lot more than
with you. He's *in* you, and He will be your guide and show you
things to come. He is moving in you right now. Take a moment
to know that He is with you and sense His peace.

Yet, even though God's Word promises the Holy Spirit is
with every Christian, the question is how often do you use your
faith to access His help, His glory, His presence? Unfortunately,
I believe perhaps it's not often enough for many of us. If only
we as Christians would draw *continually* on the grace inside of us,
we could easily defeat the devil and the many and various fiery
darts he endeavors to shoot at us.

It's sad, but too often Christians live their lives behind the
devil, which was certainly never God's plan. Jesus, the Head of
the Church, empowers us, and the Holy Spirit equips and anoints
us to live in front of the devil. Ephesians 1:22 says that the devil
has been put under the feet of Jesus, and Ephesians 2:4-5 goes on
to say that "God…hath quickened us together with Christ…and
hath raised us up together, and made us sit together in heavenly
places in Christ Jesus" (KJV).

So if the devil shows up with a truckload of trouble, we
need to look at him and say, "Listen here, bucko, God has gone
before you. Too bad for you. You are down and out. Whatever
you're trying to hand me has already been taken care of, and
you've been defeated. That's right. So hit the road, bucko."

As God's sons and daughters, we don't need to play catch
up for most of our lives. Too often for too many Christians
the scenario is this. Something catches us off guard today, and
then we pull our faith out of storage and use our faith to get
out of trouble. Our God is merciful and will always respond to
our faith, but it's clearly not God's best to only rescue us from

trouble. That puts us in a position of going through life putting out fires instead of preventing them.

God's plan is that every single day the Holy Spirit leads us to a supply of him. God's best for us is a daily provision to teach us, strengthen us, guide us and prepare us to overcome and walk in victory continually. I could tell story after story after story of how following the promptings of the Holy Spirit has delivered victory into the hands of God's children.

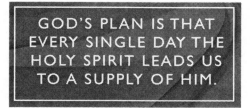

GOD'S PLAN IS THAT EVERY SINGLE DAY THE HOLY SPIRIT LEADS US TO A SUPPLY OF HIM.

Yet, the key to continual victory is living a *lifestyle of faith* as opposed to using our faith to put out emergency fires here and there. God wants you and me ready for what comes, equipped for what comes. He wants you well able to meet challenges head on and overcome them with victory permeating every area of your life.

RECEIVING YOUR DAILY PROVISION

How do you receive this daily provision God has marked for you? You receive your portion by cultivating the awareness of God in you and by talking to Him. Out of your heart, you simply begin saying, "I just love you, Holy Spirit." Perhaps you are working away on your computer or driving your truck. Whatever you're doing and wherever you're going, begin to cultivate His presence.

Tell Him, "I love You, Lord. I love You. You're the greater One in me. You're the answer I need. You're the help I need. You're working in me both to will and to do your good pleasure. You're separating me from unclean and profane things so I thank You, Lord. Oh, I love You. I love You. I love You."

It's so important that you begin to recognize Him in your life and connect with His presence inside you. Acknowledge Him and say aloud, "You're my helper. You're my guide. You always show me things to come. I believe today that I have the thoughts of You. I believe You are giving me Your thoughts and causing my thoughts to become agreeable with Your will.

> **GOD THE HOLY SPIRIT IS NOT A PLACE WE COME TO AND LEAVE; HE IS A DIVINE PERSON IN US AND WITH US WHO NEVER LEAVES US.**

thank You, Holy Spirit, that You're showing me things to come. I thank You that You're speaking to me. Thank You that You're moving in me, and leading me and guiding me in the good and the right way to go."

Do you meet with Him every day? If not, begin right there drawing closer to Him, and begin each day ever after with Him. Perhaps that's what has been missing in your life.

After all, He has invited you to meet with Him. I've learned when I start the day with Him and soak in His presence, *then* I can leave that place of prayer in His presence or fellowship and *take Him with me all day long ever aware of His presence in me. Then*, from that position I begin to release my faith to walk out the day carrying His presence into every situation and circumstance I encounter.

During these times of fellowship as we go with Him through the pages of God's Word or as He speaks to our hearts, we take a new measure and impartation of Him. That is our supply, and it's by that supply we live and move and have our being in Him day by day.

Still very aware of Him, we may bump up on a need on the path of life, and what will we do? We will simply tap inside to the God inside of us because we know every answer lies in Him, and He's in us. From our daily supply we have something to contribute to everyone we meet wherever we are and whatever we're doing that day. Perhaps it may be someone at your job or in your own family or a perfect stranger you'll be able to help because of the God supply in you.

Unfortunately, too many times as believers we do something altogether different. We take time to pray and get in the Word, but then we leave the presence of God and depend on *our own* strength to meet the needs of the day. In other words, we partake of the Word and the Spirit, but then we walk off in the natural to bring about the solutions ourselves. How many of us can testify from experience that method doesn't work? Of course it doesn't work—it's not God's plan. He never intends for us to get in to His presence and leave Him behind to handle our days without Him.

God the Holy Spirit is not a place we come to and leave; He is a divine person in us and with us who never leaves us.

So after our time in prayer and the Word, God expects us to get up from worshipping and praying and studying the Word and say, "Let's meet the day together, Holy Spirit. We'll overcome together. With Your help, I'm equipped for everything that comes my way today. With Your help, I've got the answers I need. With Your help, I've got the wisdom I need and the strength and everything else. Let's go Holy Spirit, You and me together."

Too often Christians endeavor to walk by faith without walking in the spirit. They attempt to work *spiritual* principles and formulas without the *Spirit*. In other words, they attempt to work spiritual formulas without being led by the Holy Spirit step by step into the experience of victory. The Holy Spirit is a person—not a formula. And He is alive in us to accompany us always.

Jesus Himself has said, Without Him, I can do nothing. (John 5:19). And what can we do without Him?

We simply cannot walk successfully in this life by our own reasoning or in our own strength and power. Even if we know the truth of God's Word, we still need the Spirit of God quickening that Word to us and sustaining us in life. He is the agent of grace who empowers us to overcome in this life, and it's in our union with Him that we'll know sweet victory.

It's the job of the Holy Spirit to get you ready for what's ahead. He's your personal guide. For instance, He might prompt and instruct you by witnessing to your heart, *Start reading healing scriptures and build yourself up.* Why? The Holy Spirit might see something ahead that the enemy would try and throw at you. That's one of His jobs after all—showing you things to come. The Holy Spirit is always in front as our guide, leading us with the light.

If you acknowledge and follow that guidance, you'll be built up and strengthened in God. Then, because you're strengthened in God, you're ready for whatever trouble or symptoms the devil throws your way. You'll be ready to stand strong in the truth of healing against any symptom and declare in faith, "Devil, throw your best shot at me." That may scare some of you, but if you know what you've got on the inside of you, then you know it's enough to take the enemy down every time.

> YOU ARE NOT TRYING TO GET GOD TO MEET YOUR NEEDS; HE ALREADY HAS MET YOUR NEEDS.

The Bible says you win, Church. You are not trying to get God to meet your needs; He *already has* met your needs. The Bible says in 2 Peter 1:3-4, "As His divine power *has given to us* all things that pertain to life and godliness, through the knowledge of Him who called us by glory and virtue, by which have been given to us *exceedingly great and precious promises,* that through these you may be partakers of the divine nature, having escaped the corruption that is in the world through lust" (NKJV).

The Bible is full from beginning to end of "exceedingly great and precious promises," and you need only to add your faith to receive what Jesus Christ already has provided for you. Listen, Church. The Bible says that Jesus took your infirmities and bore your sicknesses (Matthew 8:17 NKJV). The Bible says, "For whatever is born of God overcomes the world. And this is the victory that has overcome the world—our faith" (1 John 5:4 NKJV). The Bible says, "…Amid all these things we are more than conquerors and gain a surpassing victory through Him Who loved us" (Romans 8:37). The Bible says, "…God shall supply all your need according to His riches in glory by Christ Jesus" (Philippians 4:19 NKJV).

Church, you're not trying to get healed; you *are* healed. You are not trying to overcome; you *are* an overcomer. You are not trying to conquer; you *are* more than a conqueror. You are not trying to get God to meet your needs; He has *already met* your needs according to His riches in glory by Christ Jesus.

The devil has pulled a coup on the Church and endeavored to rob God's children of what rightfully belongs to them and *already has been provided* for them. Yes, the devil wants to overtake the Church and deceive many. In fact, he's deceived many devout Christians by persuading them to do the right things the wrong way. He persuades Christians to attempt to work spiritual principles in the power of the flesh. Worse yet, he's deceived Christians into working and laboring to obtain the spiritual blessings we already have been given.

But here's the truth. By faith in the blood of Jesus, you don't have to yield to the devil's deceptions. You don't have to yield to the religious busy work the devil sends your way trying to get you to earn what already belongs to you through Jesus Christ. *You don't have to work for what is already yours because it is already yours.* You only have to know what belongs to you and receive it. Faith doesn't try. Faith believes and speaks what the Word of God says belongs to you as an heir of God and joint heir of Jesus Christ.

Think about that for a minute. Think how mean and deceptive the devil is. The devil tries to convince Christians that they need to work and work and try and try to obtain their rightful inheritance. Yet, Jesus already got it back for us and gave it to us.

It all comes down to this: The devil is trying to play keep away with you.

But the Holy Spirit is on the inside of you guiding you to victory. So be careful to listen up! He'll tell you, "Build yourself up in some prosperity scriptures today." If you listen to Him, you'll be ready for that old devil. If the Holy Spirit is telling you to read prosperity scriptures, it's because He knows the enemy's plans to throw financial obstacles at you. The Holy Spirit is preparing you to win. He's on your side; He's the One helping you, guiding you and leading you to victory. He's guiding you and leading you in the good fight of faith and the right way to go. And He only knows one way—straight to victory.

The Holy Spirit is always busy with His assignment to lead and guide the Church into all truth, but the problem is that some Christians respond by saying, "Aw, I'm tired today. Well, I don't think I want to read that today. I'm too busy. I've heard that before anyway." Or, "I had something else I wanted to check out today. My favorite television show is on." OK then, do something else; it's your choice.

But if you want to live filled and flooded with the presence of God—if you want to live in His daily supply and provision for you—then it's best to do what He says. Follow your leader, the Holy Spirit, and He'll lead you right on into victory and triumph in every area of life. *His presence changes everything.*

CHAPTER **6**

CULTIVATING HIS PRESENCE

I n this hour the Holy Spirit is filling the Church with His presence; He's continually filling you and me with His presence. Every day we should be welcoming Him and rising up to another level of glory and not only in our church services, but also in our daily lives. We must walk on with God in a new way, accessing and cultivating His presence day by day. That's how we must live in this last day. It must become our way of life, an actual step-by-step walk because our Father always leads us in progression.

He always lifts us higher and higher, from glory to glory. That's how it's supposed to go. He progressively leads us in our spirits and our hearts, taking us from glory to glory to glory. But clearly, the progression is in our spirits—not our heads. Sometimes we try to obtain more and more knowledge, but yet, it's the progression in our spirits that takes us where we need to go. It's the progression in our spirits that enables the Holy

Spirit to take us to new places in God. In fact, the spirit realm is dimensional. He keeps taking us upward into more of His light and His presence.

Consider this. There's no stagnant place in God, so every day you're either increasing or decreasing in Him. Even if you don't decrease by very much, if you decrease slowly day by day in six months or a year's time you'll be far from where you were. You will be way back from where you are even now, and that's not God's best.

WE MUST WALK ON WITH GOD IN A NEW WAY, ACCESSING AND CULTIVATING HIS PRESENCE DAY BY DAY.

God only has one direction, and He only wants you moving one direction—toward Him. If you're looking for direction, I can help; God wants you moving upward and forward because He always moves higher and forward. We're not supposed to go backward or look backward. No, we're to be reaching forward toward the many different levels in God where He's invited us and welcomed us. Especially in this day we must reach from glory to glory.

Yet, take note. No matter how much we might desire to walk a different way, it takes more than "want to" or desire to make it happen. A person cannot simply say, "I will grow this year more than I ever have before," but then continue walking through life as before. In order to walk a new way, a person must make a decision to walk differently and then actually walk differently.

The very crux of the matter is this: *Decisions determine destiny, and choices determine changes.*

In order to grow and progress in the presence of God and walk in a greater degree of His presence, we must strengthen our "inner man." How is our spirit or inner person strengthened? We are strengthened as we read God's Word, confess or speak His Word, pray in other tongues and enjoy the manifest presence of God. These are the very basics that we never grow out of and we continually need to strengthen and sustain our inward being.

STRENGTHEN YOUR SPIRIT

Let me share with you specific and practical instruction that the Spirit of God has ministered to me to help strengthen your spirit and help you increase in Him. The Spirit of God is our teacher continually and desires to show us how to cultivate His presence more and more.

First of all, He's shown me to meditate day and night in the Word of God. God's Word instructs all of us in Joshua 1:8, which says, "This law book you shall never cease to have on your lips; you must pore over it day and night, that you may be mindful to carry out all that is written in it, for so shall you make your way prosperous, so shall you succeed" (Moffatt's Translation).

Friend, in my more than 30-year walk with the Lord, it's the Word of God that the Holy Spirit reveals to my heart that steadies my soul. It's imperative for us to be thoroughly—regularly and daily—nourished in the Word so we can grow in God. It's the spiritual food or bread every believer needs to "eat" in order for his or her spirit to grow and thrive. Jesus said in Matthew 4:4, "…'Man shall not live by bread alone, but by every word that proceeds from the mouth of God'" (NKJV).

It always kind of amazes me that we'll naturally feed our physical bodies food every single day and wouldn't think of depriving it of food, but some Christians go considerable lengths of time without eating spiritually. Our bodies speak loudly when they're hungry, and we do whatever it takes to feed them. But some folks deprive their spirits so long there is no spiritual strength left to overcome the enemy. Fellowship with the Word and the Spirit keep our spirits in dominion and empowered to overcome in this life.

Perhaps there are people so fortunate as to hire a live-in cook or hire someone to professionally prepare and deliver their meals. Still, I'm sure even with a chef on-site that nobody actually feeds these individuals their meals bite by bite. We must do that for ourselves. Likewise, God holds us responsible to feed ourselves spiritually as well. Remember, we are spirit, and God's Word is food for our spirits.

God's words "...are life to those who find them, healing and health to all their flesh" (Proverbs 4:22). His words are the bread of life for us to "eat" every single day. As much as we need natural bread to live, we must also have spiritual bread to live. The increase you want to see in your life will come from a strong, well-nourished spirit that feeds on and fellowships with God's Word daily.

Secondly, God has strongly witnessed to my heart the importance of praying in tongues. When you pray in tongues, 1 Corinthians 14:2 says you speak mysteries or divine secrets unto God. You pray out the plan of God, praying specifics about your life and the lives of others as well. You're praying out what's necessary for God to move in the earth and in people's lives to set things aright. John 14:13-14 says that there's nothing He will not do, if you will ask Him and believe Him.

Jude 20 tells says, "But you, beloved, build yourselves up [founded] on your most holy faith [make progress, rise like an edifice higher and higher], praying in the Holy Spirit." There's no question that we all need to keep ourselves edified and built up in the spirit to walk in His presence.

Prayer, through fellowship with Him, is also an excellent way to learn to follow the Holy Spirit. It's necessary that we get over in the spirit realm to follow Him in prayer because God is a spirit. Therefore, the more we work in those realms of prayer, the more we get to know Him, the better we get to know Him and the more we learn how to follow Him. We learn that it's impossible to follow Him out of our heads because God isn't in our heads.

The spirit realm is a real place to be accessed by following the Holy Spirit. Paul said in Ephesians 6:18 "praying always with all prayer and supplication in the spirit" (NKJV). Where did Paul tell us to pray? In what realm? He clearly told us to pray in the spirit realm. In other words, Paul is telling us to pray supernaturally. *You'll always know you are in the spirit when you become more aware of Him and His presence than the problem facing you or even your natural surroundings.*

Jesus Himself lived a life of prayer and followed the anointing in Him. As Jesus fellowshipped with the Holy Spirit, He connected Himself to the seeings and knowings of God and then the Spirit led Him successfully into every area of life and ministry. That's also how the Holy Spirit wants us to learn and to follow Him in every area of our lives and ministries.

I'm telling you, Church, there's coming a real distinction between those who pray and those who don't. For years and years, there are those who have believed that only certain people are called to pray. Yet, my mandate from God for 13 years was to take the spirit of prayer to the churches. That's what God called me to do. God called me out of my comfortable nest and sent me on down the road, saying, "You are coming upon dark hours, and the Church must know how to pray."

Yet, as I would teach and demonstrate prayer, so often I would be confronted with people saying, "Well, of course you pray because it's your call and your grace to pray."

"Hmmm … where do you find that in the Word of God?" I would respond. "Every book the apostle Paul wrote he wrote to the *Church*, and in every book he talked to the *Church* about praying." That means Paul talked to all of us about praying. The

Holy Spirit is the Spirit of Grace and Supplication, and He lives in every believer.

Brother Hagin, a mighty prophet of God, gave an untold number of prophesies by the Holy Spirit through the years calling the Church to pray. In fact, he said on many occasions that those who don't know how to pray in these last days before Jesus returns will seem to be "forlorn and forsaken." I believe those words were from the heart of God to His people. Yet, in spite of God's directive, many people hope someone else will pray for them, someone else will find the time to pray, someone else will contend for God's plans in the earth. However, I don't believe even the people who hope for someone to come along and do their praying for them actually believe that will happen.

Prayer is our connection with God, and it's so important in this hour. I believe every Christian feels called and prompted to pray deep in his or her heart even though there are those who have responded to His calling in their hearts more than others. But the Holy Spirit is always prompting and calling all of us to pray.

He's calling *you* to pray.

He's calling the Church to pray—*now!*

In fact, Jesus called His house a house of prayer for all nations (Mark 11:17). It is the call of God to the Church to be a house of prayer. Each of our churches may have different assignments of prayer from God, but we are all collectively called a house of prayer for all nations.

Thirdly, one of the most important things I believe the Holy Spirit is teaching us in this hour is to cultivate the presence of God in our lives. I've found that I absolutely cannot live without the manifest presence of God. When I say *manifest presence* of God, I mean personally experiencing God and His presence. There's a part of God I know through the Word, but there's a part of God I know because I've experienced His manifest presence in my life. It's a whole different place of knowing Him, and ultimately, it makes all the difference in your life. Truly … His presence changes everything.

EXPERIENCING GOD

We all have many relationships in our lives, and obviously we know some people better than others. In some cases we only know about someone, or perhaps we associate with a person occasionally at church, at work or at school. In other cases there are people we're really close to, and we actually experience them in our lives.

When we really experience someone—we know intimate details about the person. We know his or her likes and dislikes and thoughts and feelings. We enjoy oneness with the person because we have each shared ourselves; we have fellowshipped and communed and a deep bond has developed and joined us together. I want to *really experience* God, don't you?

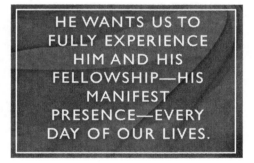

HE WANTS US TO FULLY EXPERIENCE HIM AND HIS FELLOWSHIP—HIS MANIFEST PRESENCE—EVERY DAY OF OUR LIVES.

Imagine a husband and wife living together without ever experiencing the presence of each other. There would be something missing in that relationship, wouldn't there? Imagine if the husband or wife had only read stories about the other person. Imagine if they only spoke and communicated a few seconds here and there? Would that be a close relationship of quality? Of course not, and it's the same with God and us. He wants us to fully experience Him and His fellowship—His manifest presence—*every day of our lives.*

Experiencing God should not be something that only

happens when we go to church. Of course it certainly can and should happen when we go to church; we should experience God often there. While I worship in church, God often drops answers to questions in my heart that I wasn't even considering. He speaks to all of us in church, and He loves to do that. There are times when we are worshipping and praising God in church when He will manifest Himself to us and bless our lives.

I pray everyone has rich experiences with God during church. I love those intimate times when we come together with those He joined us to in the body of Christ through His blood. He comes to us because we come to Him in worship out of our hearts, and, oh, how He moves on us and gives back to us in special ways.

And yet, we must not allow church to be the extent of our relationship and fellowship with God. In order to live and move in more and more of God's presence, we must also cultivate His presence in our lives individually as we've discussed. Church is designed to enhance and complete our personal fellowship with the Greater One, but never become a substitute for it. After all, He's the One we come to church to meet. He's the One who gave Himself for us. He's the One who lives in us. He is the One who is all wisdom, the only wise eternal and immortal God. He alone is our Father, our Leader, the Almighty One we serve and worship with our every breath.

Living in such rich individual and daily fellowship in God's presence will cause our times of coming together in church to be even more wonderful experiences in His presence. In fact, God expects us to overflow with His Spirit personally and then overflow corporately. As a pastor, I always tell our people that there are particular things God can do in our lives only when we meet corporately together as His people. There are things we can do for the advancement of His kingdom when we meet corporately that could never happen apart from one another.

How blessed is the corporate anointing and all it connects us to for the purpose of growing and experiencing more of His light and manifest presence in our lives.

Our relationship with our Father is enhanced in both individual and corporate fellowship, and it's our privilege to meet Him in both places. He is oh so satisfying and fulfilling to our hearts. Moreover, He desires for each one of His sons and daughters to know Him intimately and to experience Him in all of His wonderful attributes. He is a personal and intimate God.

We're not talking of some dried up dead God who cannot begin to relate to your life. He's not dry and boring and dead. I've heard people say, "God is just boring to me." My immediate response is simply, "Then you just do not know Him. You have not yet experienced Him. You have not yet experienced the manifest presence of God or you could never find anything about Him less than wonderful and exciting.

In one respect the anointing of God is always with us and inside us because He dwells in every born again believer. Yet, surely at times you have felt the manifest presence of God and realized it can be so real and so tangible. Perhaps you've been in prayer and His presence filled the room. Perhaps you've been in a church service, where the whole atmosphere in the room changed and seemed to become electric with His presence. Perhaps you have been in a service where the very air was charged with anointing, and His presence seemed so tangible that you felt you could cut it with a knife. Suddenly you became aware that God filled the building and changed the atmosphere—everything changed in His presence.

How true that is always. God's presence changes everything. Even now God is here while you're reading this book, and I believe He will make Himself real to you. I believe as a result you will never be the same again. Hallelujah!

For years now we've been praying and believing for a move

of God, and here it is upon us. This whole move of God is all about the glory of God and the manifest presence of God pouring out everywhere—our lives, our homes, our jobs, our cities, our schools—everywhere through us. God is real; God is alive. He's not a God for you to know from afar; He's a God who wants you and me to personally and intimately know Him.

CHANGED BY HIS PRESENCE

When I was on the staff at our home church in Nashville, Tennessee, one of my responsibilities was to do some of the counseling. People often came with complicated or sad or heart-rending situations, and I wanted to help them with all my heart. Yet, as much as I wanted to help people, I was challenged early on to learn that often I did not have the answers they needed.

There are as many needs as there are people and both are complicated. The real truth is that most people need answers that another person cannot give; people need answers that no other person has. Have you ever tried to help a friend or family member in need, but realized you didn't have the answer? We all have.

CHANGE COMES QUICKLY IN THE PRESENCE OF GOD.

The Holy Spirit taught me an important lesson in this regard. He said to me, "If you just get people to Me, I will change them." There's so much truth to that statement. I've *tried* to change many people, but it never works. You, too, probably have tried to change people, but whether you have tried or not, here's a great revelation: You cannot change people, and they cannot change you. But there is One who can.

Change comes quickly in the presence of God. I've seen people's whole lives totally turned around by the manifest presence of God. People go free of addictions, emotional and physical abuse, and so many, many problems. There's nothing quite like getting into the manifest presence of God. How come it is we don't spend more time in the life-changing, powerful, glorious presence of God?

The Spirit of God always has the answers; He's always got the help you need. He's always your Advocate, Helper, Intercessor, Standby and Comforter. He's always on your side and ready to help you. I'm sure there have been times in your life, like mine, when you've needed help or comfort. Like me you probably tried to get people to help, and it just didn't work; it wasn't enough. But there's Someone who can go deep enough to help you, and His name is the Holy Spirit.

He's here right now while you're reading. How do I know? Because I'm talking right now about you needing comfort, so I know He's here to comfort you. Press in even now because only the Holy Spirit can go deep enough to bring you the comfort you so desire. His name is the Comforter, and He comforts ever so personally. I believe some of you reading this now need His comfort. So stop reading for a minute and draw in. Begin to say, "Holy Spirit, You're my comforter. I receive You. Only You can go as deep as the comfort I need."

Only the Spirit of Comfort can reach where you are and deliver exactly what you need.

Draw in and receive. He can comfort you precisely in the way you need it the most. Draw from *Him*. If you look to yourself, you can come up empty. If you look to other people, they can disappoint. But, Church, I know One who delivers exactly what you need every time, and He's so ready and so able and so willing and so gracious to comfort you.

I can truly say that the Holy Spirit is my best friend; by His grace my life is intertwined with Him. I encourage you to become intimate with the Holy One. Allow Him to be your closest and most intimate friend—your standby. Allow the Holy Spirit to be your best friend. Allow Him to be your everything in manifestation and in reality. Don't simply know Him in theory or in doctrine or by someone else's description, but know Him personally and in reality for yourself.

> HE IS DRAWING THE CHURCH TO HIMSELF IN THIS HOUR SO WE DON'T SIMPLY KNOW THE DOCTRINE OF REDEMPTION, BUT SO THAT WE LIVE IN THE EXPERIENCE OF REDEMPTION.

Dear Church, the Holy Spirit is calling us. He is drawing the Church to Himself in this hour so we don't simply know the doctrine of redemption, but so that we live in the experience of redemption.

He desires that we have redemption in manifestation and in demonstration.

He desires that redemption be seen upon us.

Hallelujah!

God is so real. He's not religious. Actually, the more you come to know Him, the more you will realize that He's not the least bit religious; there's nothing about Him that's religious. He's honest and straight and true; He directs Himself to the real heart of every issue. He's love; He's wisdom; He's all that's good and God. Moreover, He's the Spirit who lives in me, and the Spirit who lives in you if you're born again. He's the Spirit of God, the Spirit of Christ, the anointed One, and His anointing resides on the inside of us.

He's so amazing. He's everything we need. He's the very thing we need to put us over in life. He's the answer in every situation. He's the provision for every financial need. He's the healing in every body. He's the source of every solution. And He loves you and wants to draw near to you as the personal and intimate friend that He is.

CHAPTER 7

INTIMATELY KNOWING GOD

From the moment I was baptized in the Holy Spirit many years ago, I wanted to fellowship more and more with God. Even though I had just met Him and didn't know Him, I so wanted to know Him. I wanted to *really know* Him. Of course, I knew about Him and had read about Him and heard many wonderful messages about God and about Jesus, but that simply was not enough for me.

I was so hungry for more of God that I wanted to know how to fellowship with Him, how to approach Him and what to do when I did. I wanted to know what He liked and what He didn't. Isn't that how we are when we love somebody? That should be our relationship with the Spirit of God—a love fellowship, not a religious relationship. It should be based on the knowledge of His Word and the experience—the heart knowing—that He loves us, and we love Him.

Actually back then, I didn't understand how much He desires our fellowship and intends for us to walk with Him. Now I realize that fellowship with Him is the most important thing in our lives—it *is* our lives. Why? Everything that God blesses in our lives will come out of our fellowship with Him. If we don't have a personal, one-to-one fellowship with our Father, we will only be doing what we see somebody else do and that simply won't do. What worked for others may not work for us. He made us all unique and designed us to be who we are.

God wants to communicate and fellowship with *you*. I promise if you press in far enough and enjoy true fellowship with God, it will get to you like an addiction. He will touch your spirit and soul in a way nothing else can. You'll find yourself no longer willing to live without intimacy with Him, and you'll be hungry for more and more and more of Him. Then from out of that fellowship with Him will flow everything you need and everything you want in this life and in the next. There is always more of Him to receive.

HUNGRY FOR MORE

I believe you have a hunger to know Him better and more intimately because He's drawn you to this book. I'm sure you don't simply want to know about Him, but you also want to know Him more and more. That's also my heartfelt desire, and we're in good company because the apostle Paul felt the same way.

Paul said, "[For my *determined purpose* is] that I may *know* Him [that I may progressively become more *deeply* and *intimately acquainted* with Him, perceiving and *recognizing and understanding the wonders of His Person* more strongly and more clearly], and that I may in that same way come to know the power out flowing from His resurrection [which it exerts over believers], and that I may so share His sufferings as to be continually transformed [in spirit into His likeness even] to His death, [in the hope]" (Philippians 3:10).

Read the scripture a few times and consider its living words. I particularly love Paul's phrase, *"This is my determined purpose ...."* It wasn't Paul's obligation or his Christian duty to know Him. No, no. It was so much more. Intimately knowing the Father was the purpose in his life, the focus of his heart, the very reason he lived. Did it serve Him well in His relationship with God? I would say so. Paul knew God intimately—well enough to write much of the New Testament and take the gospel message to most of the known world in his day.

People who are hungry for more of God sometimes think, *If only I had been living in Bible days then I could know Jesus better.* Yet, Paul lived after the time of Jesus' earthly ministry and knew Jesus by revelation. That means Paul knew Him the same way we can know Him. Paul had a revelation of the living God in him. He had the revelation of "Christ in me, the hope of glory." It gave Paul boldness and confidence to do impossible things. It gave him boldness and confidence to shake cities and shake nations.

Let's face it, you won't shake a nation or a city with doctrine and neither will I. It simply won't work. If that approach worked—if doctrine alone could get the job done—the Church would have accomplished it long ago. All nations and cities would have been reached; we would have reached the uttermost

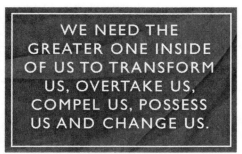

WE NEED THE GREATER ONE INSIDE OF US TO TRANSFORM US, OVERTAKE US, COMPEL US, POSSESS US AND CHANGE US.

and completed our Great Commission.

Doctrine is vital and necessary, but it won't shake anything. What is needed is something—Someone—in us who's greater than we are. We need the Greater One inside of us to transform

71

us, overtake us, compel us, possess us and change us. We need the Greater One who will enable us and equip us to boldly and powerfully demonstrate the greater works of the gospel before people's eyes. We need Someone working with us to confirm the Word of God with signs, wonders and miracles. We need the Spirit of God demonstrating God's Word by raising the dead, healing bodies, causing limbs to grow and so much more.

We need to *know* God so He can do exploits through us. We have God's Word on that in Daniel 11:32, which says, "...The people that do know their God shall be strong, and do *exploits*" (KJV). The Spirit of God is ever ready to demonstrate with might and power, and that's why we must take the God inside of us to the multitudes. He wants to do His work in our lives and then move out of us into this seen realm for people to see and know He is alive.

Church, if we *know Him* we won't wonder if sick people will be healed when we pray. We won't wonder if limbs will grow when we pray because we *know* the living God; we know the Greater One in us. If we know Him, we won't go lay hands on people because a pastor or a Bible school or anyone else instructed us to do so; He will personally move in and upon us with His power and glory. If we know Him, He will compel us to minister to the sick with an anointing to heal, deliver and set people free. If we know Him, we will demonstrate that Jesus is alive and His resurrection power is in us. Glory to God!

Listen to what the Holy Spirit is saying in this hour, Church. The Holy Spirit is saying, "Wake up! Come on, Church. Wake up and let me take hold of you. Receive the revelation and the truth that Christ is in you, and you're filled with His anointing. Let's shake off religion. Shake off those old dead things that keep you wondering and wondering and talking and talking about the supernatural life that you cannot quite attain. Shake off the focus of tomorrow, and rise up today."

This is the day the Lord has prepared you and me for; this

is the hour for the Church to rise. Glory to God, the Holy One has empowered you and me to live victoriously on this earth all the while living in His presence and fully experiencing Him. He has called us to reign in life by Christ Jesus.

You cannot tell me He doesn't heal. It's too late. I've experienced it. You can't tell me He doesn't prosper people because I've experienced His prosperity. You cannot tell me He doesn't do miracles; I've experienced Him and His miracles. When there wasn't a way, He made a way. It's too late to tell me otherwise. You simply cannot tell

> GLORY TO GOD, THE HOLY ONE HAS EMPOWERED YOU AND ME TO LIVE VICTORIOUSLY ON THIS EARTH ALL THE WHILE LIVING IN HIS PRESENCE AND FULLY EXPERIENCING HIM.

me there's anything He cannot do because I know Him. *I know Him!* ***I know Him!***

Here is the best part, dear friend. When you're hungry to know Him, He'll make Himself known. When you're thirsty for Him, He will quench your thirst. When you desire Him more than the air you breathe, He will meet you at the point of your desire. That is the job of the Holy Spirit. It's His job to satisfy you, and it's your job to live satisfied. Don't be satisfied only craving more of Him; be satisfied living filled to the full. Be satisfied by living in His presence.

Ephesians 5:17-18 says, "Wherefore be ye not unwise, but understanding what the will of the Lord is, and be not drunk with wine, wherein is excess; but be filled with the Spirit" (KJV). That word *filled* in the Greek means a continuing state of being filled, to go on being filled, or literally, *be being filled*. There is a difference between eating and eating until you're full. There's a difference between taking a drink of water and having your thirst quenched. There's a difference between visiting and enjoying the presence of God and living fully satisfied in the presence of God. In this hour, we are being called to live full of His presence, fully satisfied and intertwined with Him. We are called to be in union and oneness with Him.

Then—and only then—we are ready to let Him be made known through us so that we don't stand in front of sick, hurting and desperate people wavering and saying, "I wonder if this person will get set free if I pray. Oh God, You better show up." Instead we'll stand boldly knowing that our God will manifest to set people free because He shows up every time we pray. We know because we know *Him*.

CHAPTER **8**

MARKED BY FELLOWSHIP

What we have seen and ourselves heard, we are also telling you, so that you too may realize and enjoy fellowship as partners and partakers with us. And this fellowship that we have which is a distinguishing mark of Christians is with the Father and with His Son Jesus Christ (the Messiah).—*1 John 1:3*

How glorious that our Creator—our Father—is inviting us to intimately and continually fellowship with Him. He's inviting us to draw near to Him and truly know Him, and from out of that fellowship flows supernatural provision and destiny. He is the distinguishing mark of Christians; He is the distinguishing mark in your life and mine. He has marked us in the realm of the spirit.

From out of our fellowship with God flows guidance and direction in every circumstance and situation that comes our way. He gives us the when and the how, and then He helps us walk out the solution. Too often we receive spiritual principles or supernatural wisdom from God, but then we try to walk them out naturally. That's never how God intended our Christian walk to be.

He intends to impart directions and answers to us, and then walk them out together with us. God intends for us to be dependent on Him, connected with Him and intertwined with Him. That is His plan, and it's so much better and so much higher than where we've walked as a body and a Church up until this point.

Listen, Church, God stands ready to help us and provide every answer we need. God is for us. He's on our side, and He's speaking to us even now. Let's turn our hearts to hear.

He's not far. He's near. He's here—as close as your own heart or spirit.

ROOMS OF GOD

All of the places of God are inside us and in us can be found all of the rooms of God. But, dear Church, as mentioned earlier I'm not talking about a physical place where we go or arrive. Rather, I'm talking about a place of the heart or a position on the inside of us—a position *in Him*. The Bible says in Acts 17:28 that in Him we live and move and have our being. How true. *In Him* we live and move. *In Him* we move. *In Him in us*, we move. *In Him in us*, we live. *In Him in us*, we have our being. Hallelujah.

I've learned that if we'll arrive at this place of oneness and continual fellowship with Him, then what He's able to do in our lives every single day is truly amazing. Remember, He's the One who knows all things—*everything*. There's nothing about anything anywhere anytime that He doesn't know. So be confident, then, that He knows how you can prosper in an instant. He knows how you can obtain your healing just like that. He knows how you can rise up and increase at the snap of a finger.

He has all of the answers. He has answers for questions you do not even know to ask. He has every answer you could ever need or want, and it's all inside of *you*. And as you yield to Him in fellowship, He will teach you to draw from this place of fellowship every single thing you need.

Dear friend, this place of fellowship with Him is the very thing for which your heart has cried. It's the very reason you were born, and it will satisfy you to the core of your being. His presence changes absolutely everything. As we develop and cultivate this hunger and this receptivity to know Him and to walk with Him and to experience Him,

> . . . IF WE'LL ARRIVE AT THIS PLACE OF ONE-NESS AND CONTINUAL FELLOWSHIP WITH HIM, THEN WHAT HE'S ABLE TO DO IN OUR LIVES EVERY SINGLE DAY IS TRULY AMAZING.

something marvelous happens. James 4:8 says, "Draw near to God, and He will draw near to you" (NKJV). But again, Church, this scripture isn't referring to drawing near in distance, but rather in experience.

If you're living off an experience you had in God 10 years ago, you're playing hooky spiritually. What is your experience today? What was your experience last week? *Every day there's a place for you to go in God.* Remember as we discussed earlier, every day He can bring you to the level of His provision for you that day. Every day He has a supply for you; He intends to impart His presence in you to equip you, guide you and anoint you to meet and handle and overcome whatever comes your way on a given day. That's who He is, and that's who He intends for you to be.

AN INVITATION TO MORE

I believe that God is endeavoring to impart something to you now. I believe He is inviting you to come up to a higher place in Him. Perhaps God is imparting to you a greater hunger for more of Him. Maybe He's calling you to a deeper place in Him. I pray it serves whatever purpose He desires for you.

Actually, there are many ways to fellowship with the Lord, and the Holy Spirit will lead you to the one that's right for you at the time. Sometimes we are led to fellowship with God through the study of His Word. Sometimes we are led to fellowship with Him through anointed music. Sometimes He leads us to study the Word of God and sing songs to Him. Sometimes He leads us to meditate

> ACTUALLY, IF WE'RE NOT CAREFUL, WE CAN SPEND TIME LEARNING ABOUT HIM OR SINGING ABOUT HIM, WHEN OUR PURPOSE IS TO COME TO KNOW HIM.

quietly. Sometimes He leads us to simply bask in His presence. All of these methods and more have their place as He leads us into more of His presence and we come to know Him more intimately.

Actually, if we're not careful, we can spend time learning *about* Him or singing *about* Him, when our purpose is to come to know *Him*. We must know Him when He's speaking and know Him when He's leading.

How can we come to know Him?

The answer is truly simple: *The only way you'll really know Him is to get into His presence and allow His presence to manifest to you personally.*

The presence of God is like an imprint on your life because He makes an imprint on you. Likewise, the Holy Spirit wants to imprint you daily with Himself; He wants to leave His mark on your life. He wants His imprint upon you to direct where you go and provide for you the supply and the substance of God to meet the day or even events coming down the road.

Let me encourage you to enter the rooms of God or the places in His presence that await you. They are inside of you. Look in. And enter in to experience and pursue your Father. Perhaps you've wondered before, *How do I fellowship with God? How do I talk to Him? I want to get close, but how do I do it?*

I can share with you how He leads me, but it's important that you realize that the way I go into His presence isn't the only way; it's only my way. Perhaps these guidelines will be a practical introduction for you or simply a refreshing, but the goal is for you to find His way for you because He's designed your way personally for you. He is a personal and intimate God.

Nevertheless, I will describe how I enter His presence as one possible scenario or pathway of fellowship. First of all, as I set my heart to enter His presence, I find a place where I can be quiet and undisturbed. I find a place where I can give my undivided attention to the Holy One, not distracted by phones, door knocks or any other interruption.

I also purpose to establish an environment not limited by anything, particularly time. I set time aside as a divine appointment with my Father, and I focus only on Him. I won't be distracted by a clock or watch; I cannot limit God by the minutes on a clock. Too often we're in too much of a hurry and busy with everything in our lives, but we cannot let that same attitude creep into our fellowship with our Father.

Another important tool for my fellowship experience is instrumental music. I find that playing anointed instrumental music helps me hook up with the presence of God and follow Him. It helps me close out the world and create an environment and atmosphere of worship. It's important to me that the music be instrumental only, so that the lyrics don't get in my way and distract me.

I always make sure to have my Bible with me as I fellowship with the Father because it contains the words His heart wants us to have. The Spirit of God moved on men of old to write the Word of God so our Father could speak to us; He is the author and so surely it contains His heart. The Bible provides us 66 books full of divine and supernatural instruction for our lives, so there's no question that the Guide Himself will direct us to its messages. In fact, many times I make a point of holding God's Word in my hands as I enjoy His presence so the Holy Spirit can lead me through its pages.

Then I begin to lift my voice to worship Him in spirit and in truth. I acknowledge Him; I connect with Him through my words. I lift my voice and worship Him like this:

Hallelujah, hallelujah. Thank You, Lord. Thank You, Holy Spirit, You're the One Jesus told me all about. You're the One who always comes to me because I ask You to, and I thank You that You're here right now. You're the guide I trust.

You're the One who always shows me things to come. You're the One that Jesus promised would never leave me and never forsake me. You're right here. You're right here living and dwelling in me. It's so comforting to know that You never leave me, no matter what I do. You're always here. I may miss it and pull away from You, but You always take me right back. I love You. I love You more today than I have in my whole life.

We've had so many times together, and You always speak to me the things You hear. So what are You hearing now? What are You hearing, Holy Spirit? Jesus promised that You wouldn't speak of Yourself, but You would always speak of Him and what You hear Him say. So what is He saying? Where do we want to go?

Holy Spirit, I know that this Word will speak to me today, and it will speak right now. Welcome Holy Spirit. Lead me through the pages of God's Word. Guide me where You want me to go. Teach me and show me. What do You hear Him say? What are You seeing Him do? What will please Him today? I love You. I trust You. I wait to hear where we're going, and I'm following You there.

I know You will take me to a place in You. You'll reveal. You'll transmit things into me, things that are inside of You. I know You will transmit them into my heart. How wonderful my inheritance is that I may come into Your presence. I love Your presence.

As I continue in His presence talking to Him, perhaps I feel prompted to turn to a certain passage or scripture in the Word. As I look there with Him, I know in my heart that the Holy Spirit is talking to me. The scripture bears witness in my heart, and I know He led me to the scripture; it contains a message to me from Him.

So immediately I continue to worship Him with the very truth He highlighted to me in my spirit. I hold the Word before Him and partake of it. Sometimes I speak it back to Him, and in my heart, I watch for a witness on a word or a phrase.

As an example of how we can worship Him in truth, let's consider that He led me to Psalm 46, which says, "God is our refuge and strength, a very present help in trouble. Therefore we will not fear, though the earth be removed, and though the mountains be carried into the midst of the sea; Though its waters roar and be troubled, Though the mountains shake with its swelling. Selah. There is a river whose streams shall make glad the city of God, The holy place of the tabernacle of the Most High. God is in the midst of her, she shall not be moved; God shall help her, just at the break of dawn. The nations raged, the kingdoms were moved; He uttered His voice, the earth melted" (verses 1-6 NKJV).

Reading over the verses, we begin to talk to the Holy Spirit saying:

> Lord, I know these are Your words to me. So, Holy Spirit, breathe into these words so they become life to me. I draw from your strength, God (verse 1). You are my refuge, and You are my strength. I draw from You right now. You are the strength that I need today. You are the strengthener, and You are my refuge. I put myself there right now.

I continue through the verses saying:

> You are always ready to help me in times of trouble (verse 1). You're always right there, and You're always ready to help. I know You'll help me. Anytime trouble comes, I know You deliver me. Thank You, thank You for being the help I need, the help I can always depend on.

> I will not fear even if earthquakes come and mountains crumble into the sea (verse 2).

> No, I'm not afraid. Even if the oceans roar and foam, and the mountains tremble (verse 3), I'm not afraid because You are my help and my refuge. You're the strength; You're the strength, the strength of my soul. You're the strength of my inner being. You strengthen my mind, and I receive it now. I love You.

> A river brings joy to the city of our God, the sacred home of the Most High (verse 4). That's the river that flows out of Your throne, and that's the river that I'm joined to that flows to and through me. All of heaven is filled with that river, and it's the same

river that is in You. It's the same river that comes out of Your throne and fills the heavenly city, and it's the same river that's in me. Wow!

God Himself lives in that city, and it can't be destroyed (verse 5). God Himself lives in me because that river is in me so I cannot be destroyed. I can never be destroyed because You're in me, and You're living there. I love You for that. I love You that You fought for that plan, and You made a way.

For thousands of years, You made a way so that today the same river in Jesus is the same river in me, and it's flowing to me. I love You for that. You protect it at the break of day, the nations are in an uproar. Kingdoms crumble, and God thunders and the earth melts (verse 6).

The Lord Almighty Himself is here among us right now. The same Lord almighty who created the heavens and the earth formed and fashioned a body for Jesus to live in so He could come. The same One is right here in us and with us. How wonderful. How wonderful, oh, You're the same. You're the same.

You're the same to me, and You're the same in me as You were in Jesus. Come see the glorious works of the Lord. You are God, and how glorious are all of your works. Show us Your works, Jesus. Let us see the glorious works of the Lord. Let us see now all the glorious works that You've planned for us.

I think about the glorious works You've done in times past—when You parted the Red Sea, when you parted the Jordan—all the things You did so your people could be free. And I think about the glorious works You did through Jesus for me. You took everything that was in me, all of my sin, and You put it in Jesus.

You put every disease and every sickness that would ever try to come upon me, every disease the earth would ever know, and You put it on Him (Isaiah 53). You put it all on Him so I could be healed. You took everything that was sin and death in and of me, and You gave it to Jesus.

Dear Jesus, I hardly even know how to say thank You enough for what You did, but you know my heart. You know what's in my heart that words alone cannot express. Yet, thank You that You made me new, and now I'm made of You. I'm made of Your righteousness and made of Your love and made of Your spirit.

I sing in the spirit now, allowing my heart to give expression and say thank You. Lift Your voice to Him now.

Dear Jesus, the same breath that breathed into You is the same breath that breathed into me and made all things new. I love You. Thank You that You loved me that much. You loved me enough to be a friend who would lay down His life for me, and I love You. Teach me more about You. Teach me more about how to hear You and how to live in You and in Your presence.

Most usually as I continue worshipping the Holy One in spirit and in truth, He begins to speak specifically to me about different matters I've held before Him. Often I will begin to receive answers to questions I have asked Him, and often I receive answers to questions I have not yet even asked Him. Being still in His presence gives His voice amplification into my spirit.

I begin to respond to Him very personally, acknowledging every detail and facet of what He's spoken to my heart by saying:

> Holy Spirit, I see, I see. I didn't know that. Thank You for speaking that to my heart. Yes, that's an answer. I appreciate that. I asked a long time ago about that. I love You. Holy Spirit, You're the all wise one, and Your wisdom comes to me.
>
> Now, Holy One, I'm bringing this other matter up to you now. It just rose up in my heart, and I'm lifting that up to You. What do you think about it? What do you say about that? What are your thoughts on it? Yes, You think it's good? OK, I'll do that. How wonderful that because of everything Jesus did, I can draw so close—so close to the place where You are in me, where your presence is. Hallelujah!

Listen quietly as His presence fills your heart, fills the room and surrounds you. Be still in His presence and reverence Him.

As I'm led forward, I begin again saying:

> God Almighty, the Creator of the universe, the One who framed the worlds with His Word, the One by whom all things consist has the Spirit of Himself dwell inside me. I am overwhelmed.
>
> Thank You, Holy Spirit, My teacher, my guide. I love You, my God, my Father. Thank You, Lord Jesus, my Master. You will be honored by every nation, and You will be honored throughout the whole world. Nations will bow to you, and You will be glorified. Hallelujah! Thank You, Lord.

In my time of fellowship, I continue praying:

> Now, Holy Spirit, You teach us to live in Your presence. This place where we abide, teach us all how to live here for the rest of our days. Teach us

of the things we must do. Teach us of the things of You that You want us to see. Teach us and train us and take us into the things of You.

I know You desire to lead us into places we've never been. So take us there; move us from the place where we are, the place where You're drawing us now. Take us to a place of oneness, a place of union and intimacy, a place where we walk with You. Take us to a place where all things wait—everything You have to give to us, it's all there. Take us to a place where everything we need, it's all there. I love You, Jesus. Now, Holy Spirit, teach us all how to know You and know You more intimately and to become more one with You than we've ever been. Hallelujah.

I love You. I love these times with You. I bless You, my God, my Lord, my Redeemer who lives in me. I love You for all the benefits I have—all my sins forgiven, all my diseases healed, every provision and protection provided and all Your goodness and mercy following me today and forever. Thank You.

Then most importantly of all, I become still and let Him speak. If there's anything else He desires to say, I entreat Him to do it. I entreat Him to search my heart and life of anything not of Him in me. I ask Him to shine His light on any area where I may need to repent.

Again, I simply sit and listen.

I have connected with Him; I have accessed His presence and fellowshipped there, so I wait there. I receive of Him in His presence, and I revel in my time with Him.

IMPARTATIONS AWAITING YOU

Dear Church, in this place of worship and fellowship is

the daily portion for your life. Only He can give you this daily portion, which will take you higher and further in God. Even more, the destiny and the plan He has for your life—everything you need to succeed and possess your spiritual inheritance—is in this place. We have such an inheritance that He's given to all of us, but the greatest inheritance that has been bestowed upon mankind is the very presence of God in and upon and toward us. How wonderful is His love for you and me.

As you go through the Word daily in God's presence, look for where the presence and unction speak to your spirit. While the entire Word of God is full of the power to bring itself to pass, you will find there will not necessarily be presence on every single word every single day or every single occasion.

But the presence will be on one word—God's word to you today. That's why you heard me go over and over about the presence, and then

> WE HAVE SUCH AN INHERITANCE THAT HE'S GIVEN TO ALL OF US, BUT THE GREATEST INHERITANCE THAT HAS BEEN BESTOWED UPON MANKIND IS THE VERY PRESENCE OF GOD IN AND UPON AND TOWARD US.

the presence or the unction fell on the word *strength*. It fell on the point that *He's my strength*. Then as I recognized where the presence or the unction or the anointing fell, I kept working with that word so the presence could work in me and equip me for where I am at the very moment the Holy Spirit is drawing me to that provision.

God wants to do the same for you. Impartations are awaiting you. So I trust He has imparted something into your heart even as you are reading this book. Again, the way He leads me is not the only way to be led. It's not even the only way He always leads me. Sometimes He leads in altogether different rivers.

Sometimes the river of presence is quiet and still. Other times I have followed a river of presence that's completely different, rolling on the floor laughing in my house all by myself alone with God. Why? Because that's where He took me that day, and it was a good thing because the joy of the Lord is our strength.

Let me share this with you. The presence of God is absolutely worth whatever price you must pay or whatever you must lay down in order to experience it. It's so worth it; there's nothing like experiencing the manifest presence of God. Once in a place of true fellowship with Him, you will learn that you don't have to leave the place without Him and leave Him behind. Did you hear me? You don't have to enter this place of fellowship and then leave Him there only to walk on by yourself.

I always use my faith and say, "Now, Holy Spirit, we have a whole day together, and we're going to walk it together." Then you just take Him with you because He'll go with you—that's His assignment. Thereby, you learn to practice and cultivate the presence of God as your daily practice—as your lifestyle.

"But if I'm born again and Spirit filled isn't the Holy Spirit already inside me and always with me?" Yes, of course He is. Remember, the presence of God is always with us, but the manifest presence of God comes as we become aware of Him, invite Him, connect with Him and cultivate His presence at all times in all places. He'll manifest in your car. He'll manifest in your truck. He'll manifest in your laundry room. He'll manifest on your job. He'll manifest in your office. He'll manifest in your classroom. And He'll do it because He loves to manifest to you, and He loves to do it all the time.

From this time on let me challenge you that we shouldn't be people who live without experiencing the manifest presence of God on a continual basis. God has said He will fill the whole earth with His glory. He will fill the earth with the manifest presence of Himself. So expect Him to manifest. Don't think He'll do it for somebody else; He wants to do it for *you.*

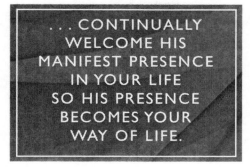

. . . CONTINUALLY WELCOME HIS MANIFEST PRESENCE IN YOUR LIFE SO HIS PRESENCE BECOMES YOUR WAY OF LIFE.

He will do it for you *whenever you expect and allow Him.*

Let me encourage you to continually welcome His manifest presence in your life so His presence becomes your way of life.

After all, Jesus paid the price so that we could walk with God and know sweet fellowship all of our days.

CHAPTER 9

ONE LIFE TO LIVE

Spending time in the presence of the Lord is so fulfilling, so amazing, so marvelous that there was a time I got way over in a ditch wanting to be with Jesus all the time to the detriment of everything else. I craved to be in the presence of God, and in response to everything else my attitude was, *Don't bother me. Don't bring me out of this place in God to do natural things.* I'd work around the house thinking, *Hurry up, clean the house. Hurry up, get the dishes done. Hurry up, get everyone out of the house so I can just be with Jesus.*

I felt as though I lived two lives. I felt as though I had a spiritual life over on one side that consisted of reading the Bible, praying, spending time with Jesus, studying and helping at the church. Then everything else was over on the other side in my natural life that consisted of being a wife and a mother, cleaning the house, ironing clothes, washing dishes, mopping, vacuuming and all of those things. I couldn't wait to get through with all the natural duties so I could get back over to the spiritual life, which is all I wanted.

At that time, I wasn't even thinking about ministry; I just wanted to hang out with Jesus. Actually, I was struggling to live two lives—*two very different lives.*

This became a problem because I had other important things to do. I had other important responsibilities and roles like taking care of my husband and my family, taking care of my house and the list goes on. Yet my heart's cry was, *Oh, Jesus, I just want to spend time with You. I just want to be with You.* But you know what? It wasn't long before I realized that I wouldn't have a family if I continued thinking that way.

Have you ever felt like that or lived like that? If not, let me tell you that it can heap a lot of stress on your life because the whole time you're over here, you want to be over there. So you begin to go through most of your life wanting to be somewhere else. Then, too, a person can get stuck thinking his or her natural life is enough, but that's certainly not true.

> YOUR SPIRITUAL LIFE EMPOWERS YOUR NATURAL LIFE AND GIVES YOU PURPOSE TO LIVE YOUR LIFE.

Your spiritual life empowers your natural life and gives you purpose to live your life. In fact, Jesus lived a supernatural life on earth, and it is also our calling to live a supernatural life on earth.

Yet, the truth is that many Christians try to divide their lives in the same way I did, which is a big hindrance. It really stunts our growth and hinders us from growing and increasing in all that is ours in Christ Jesus. Actually many Christians become thoroughly messed up trying to live two lives.

Have you found yourself thinking as I did that your spiritual life includes Bible reading, praying, church, hanging out with other Christians and doing other so called "spiritual" things? Then have you found yourself in a rut with your job, house cleaning, laundry, taking care of families and other "natural" things all the while thinking these mundane tasks are not as important as your spiritual life?

Unfortunately, if that's the case, then you're living like I was. Your life is separated into departments, and in taking care of natural affairs, you become separated from God. No wonder you are anxious and in a hurry to push your natural life out of the way in favor of growing and going on with God.

But hear me now. This isn't God's plan at all. I thank God that the Holy Spirit taught me the truth and turned my life around. If you've been endeavoring to live a double life, the Holy Spirit is about to do the same for you.

I had compartmentalized everything, and consequently, I wasn't enjoying the life I had been given. I raced to finish chores so I could fellowship with Him, and it seemed that everything suffered. But, oh, praise God, I remember the moment the Holy Spirit spoke to me and set me free. He said, "Karen, *your whole life makes a contribution to my plan in the earth.*" Suddenly I realized that my life as a mother, my life as wife and my spiritual life *all contributed* to God's plan for me and to God's plan in the earth. Suddenly I realized that God never asked me to live two lives, but rather *one whole life.*

That's how Jesus lived His life. Jesus' *whole life* was acceptable unto God; everything Jesus did pleased the Father. How do we know? Jesus said so. He said, "...the Son can do nothing of Himself, but what He sees the Father do; for whatever He does, the Son also does in like manner" (John 5:19 NKJV). Jesus also explained "...for I *always* do those things that please Him [my Father]" (John 8:29 NKJV).

Since Jesus said He always pleased the Father that would mean He pleased the Father when He was traveling with His family; Jesus pleased the Father when He was working in the carpenter's shop; and He pleased the Father when He laid hands on the sick and saw them recover. In other words, Jesus' whole life was acceptable to God. The life of the apostle Paul also pleased the Father, which would mean Paul pleased God when he was a tent maker, and Paul pleased God when He wrote the epistles we read today.

Your whole life also can please the Father and contribute to God's plan in the earth.

Of course, a young mother cannot spend hours in the presence of God and still care for babies and young children. When you have a job to go to, you cannot spend hours a day in the presence of God. Yet, it's wonderful to realize that every part of your life still contributes to the plan of God in the earth. There are times when it's more important to sow to spiritual things or to natural things, *but both contribute to the plan of God.*

Too often we condemn people because they don't pray 10 hours a day or four hours a day. The devil will always tell us that we haven't read the Bible enough and that we haven't prayed enough. He will always tell us that whatever amount of time we've sown to the spirit or to prayer isn't enough. If we prayed four hours, he would say we should have prayed five. He will always tell us that we're not doing enough no matter how much we might be doing.

But that's not what Jesus has to say. That's not what the Holy Spirit has to say. Jesus knew that even when He was helping His father in the carpenter's shop that He was contributing to the plan of God in the earth. Obviously it didn't equal the spiritual importance of divine appointments yet to come, but it was Jesus' contribution to God's plan at that moment in time. Jesus walked by the leading of the Spirit of God, and He walked in continual fellowship with His Father. He did what He saw the Father do and said what He heard the Father say.

Church, we are not called to live two different lives—it's all one life. Paul said it this way in 1 Corinthians 10:31 "…whether you eat or drink, or whatever you do, do all to the glory of God"

(NKJV). That's the key right there. Whatever you do, do it as unto the Lord. That means that you are the same person at church as you are at home. Your character should be the same at home and church as it is at work. Because you have gained this awareness that your whole life contributes to the will and the plan of God, you can begin to live one life truly devoted to God.

It's a hindrance for us to live with segmented and compartmentalized areas in our lives, so we must change our mindset and realize that our whole lives contribute to God. *The whole point is not to do natural things and spiritual things, but to do all things wholly acceptable unto God living a supernatural life.*

The devil beats people up in their thought lives because they work secular jobs or their jobs are this or that. He tries to tell people that ministers are more spiritual, but they're absolutely not. Whatever God has assigned you to do in this life *is* your ministry. The point is, your whole life can be dedicated to God— all the time, everywhere, every place and in every way.

I got in a ditch because I wanted to spend all my time with Jesus, and then the tendency was to let the natural life go. But that begins to hurt the people you love the most. So I learned to come into God's presence every day and receive in His presence, and from that place of fullness I could impart to others around me in my natural life. Every day I come into His presence and receive an impartation of love; it's always love from Him because He *is* love. Then I'm able to give His love everywhere I go, imparting God everywhere I go, and life is altogether sweet and fulfilling.

Let me encourage you to forget all about trying to live two lives—don't even try. Rather, give your whole life to God. Whether you're a wife or a husband or a mother or a father, live unto Him. Whether you're a minister or a worker or a student or a business woman or a business man, live unto Him. Make your whole life a contribution to Him. Thereby you will keep yourself ever aware of Him and ever walking with Him.

So many times I see people who graduate from Bible school become especially frustrated with their lives because they're not in the ministry or serving God the way they expected they would. But, that's a lie and a deception of the enemy because your whole life makes a contribution to God. My life as a wife was and is contributing to the plan of God in the earth. My life as a mother was and is contributing to the plan of God in my life. And no matter the call on your life, your natural life also contributes to the plan of God.

Jesus is our example in life and ministry, and His entire life from the time He was born to the time He died on the cross was a contribution to the plan of God in the earth. Everything counted. In other words, no one can deny the importance of Jesus' earthly ministry, His death on the cross and His resurrection. But Jesus' life as a boy at work in His earthly father's carpenter's shop helping with the family business was also important; those also were times and seasons of His life. Jesus' life as a youth was not something to be looked down upon.

Too often even those called to the ministry at a young age think, *Oh, I just can't wait until I grow up so I can be in ministry.* Yet, that is not how God arranged and designed our lives. God Himself orchestrated seasons; God Himself established times of growing and preparation. God knows that many experiences—some seemingly natural—intertwine to make us the person who will eventually step into the fullness of His plan. Jesus' youth made a contribution to His life just as your youth made a contribution to your life or is making to your life.

The apostle Paul said in Acts 17:28, "'For in Him we live and move and have our being ...'" (NKJV). Paul was making the point that whatever we do—whether eating, drinking, making tents, attending church or preaching—it is our whole life. And with his whole life, Paul served the Lord.

At the same time, you must realize that I'm not saying that

Paul making tents was equally as important as Paul writing much of the New Testament. Or that Jesus working in the carpenter's shop with his earthly father was equally as important as teaching and preaching and healing the sick or raising the dead. Obviously Jesus raising Lazarus from the dead was more important than pounding nails in the carpenter's shop, and obviously Paul writing the New Testament was more important than his youthful activities. No, of course, they are not of equal spiritual importance. But these seemingly mundane natural activities and seasons still do contribute to the plan of God, and it will set you free to understand this fact.

> BE THE BEST YOU CAN BE AT WHATEVER YOU'RE DOING; GIVE YOUR ALL TO ALL THAT YOU DO.

Church, this can help you. In whatever position of life you find yourself right now—whatever age, whatever phase—you are contributing to your whole life; you are contributing to the plan of God. Therefore, be the best you can be at whatever you're doing; give your all to all that you do. Serve wherever you are to the best of your ability and with excellence because that's where you are. Then in whatever phase you find yourself, you'll be contributing to your future and to God's plan, and you'll be serving God with excellence.

I see people frustrated when they don't grasp this truth. Sometimes I have to grab hold of myself and jerk myself back over into this whole life reality as well. It's easy to slip and desire to devote all your time to things of the Spirit. That's what religion wants you to do. Religion tries to persuade you that what you're doing in life is not important and not contributing to the plan of God. But, friend, that's a lie of hell.

Now if you're not serving God, that's a whole different story. If you're out sinning and doing what you want to do, then you're making no contribution at all except to hell's plan. That certainly isn't where God intends for you to be. God intends for you to live every single day, all day long *in Him* doing His will. In fact, that's God's instruction to you.

God says, "If we live by the [Holy] Spirit, let us also *walk* by the Spirit. [If by the Holy Spirit we have our life in God, let us go forward *walking* in line, our conduct controlled by the Spirit]" Galatians 5:25. That's Bible. That's the new covenant. That's truth. What hinders us in this natural life are these five physical senses that keep us unaware of God, but more aware of this world. Yet, with the help of the Word and the Spirit, we can walk in a supernatural life obedient to His will and doing His plan.

GOD IS WHERE YOU ARE

God has spoken to me so many times in so many different ways through Genesis 28, which tells the story of Jacob's ladder. I love how the chapter describes this glorious moment in this man's life. Jacob watched the angels of God ascending and descending up and down, and suddenly he realized, *God is here, and I did not even know it.*

> WE NEED TO CULTIVATE THE AWARENESS OF GOD'S PRESENCE EVERYWHERE ALL AROUND US IN ORDER TO EXPERIENCE A GREATER SPIRITUAL RECEPTIVITY AND KNOWING OF THE PRESENCE OF GOD IN US.

It's the same in your life. When you go home, God is there. When you go to bed tonight, God will be there. When you go to your kitchen, God is there. When you go to work, God is there. God is here while you're reading. No matter how far you go or where you go, God is everywhere; He is all around.

The same thing dawned on David in Psalm 139 when he said, "No matter where I go, if I go to heaven, if I go to Sheol, wherever I go, He is there. I can't get away from His presence. I can't get away from God." How true! That's the very awareness we need to cultivate. We need to cultivate the awareness of God's presence everywhere all around us in order to experience a greater spiritual receptivity and knowing of the presence of God in us. God's presence is always with us all day long, every single day no matter what we're doing. It's religion that would have you segregate your life. Religion likes to box God into one small corner of our lives.

People often ask me this question: How many hours a day do you pray? They look forward to my answer because I've traveled for many years preaching and teaching on prayer in churches and imparting a spirit of prayer into the body of Christ. Usually it surprises people when I answer, "I don't establish a certain amount of prayer time each day; other days I may pray all day long." I pray as the Holy Spirit *leads me* and *prompts me* to pray.

LED BY PROMPTINGS

Let's look at Romans 7 to see how we new covenant believers can make our prayer lives and our entire natural lives spiritual. It's a principle that will lead us into a greater increase in God. Verse 6 says, "But now we have been delivered from the law, having died to what we were held by, *so that we should serve in the newness of the Spirit and not in the oldness of the letter*" (NKJV).

Notice how The Amplified Bible translates the verse and particularly the last sentence: "But now we are discharged from the Law and have terminated all intercourse with it, having died to what once restrained and held us captive. So now we serve not under [obedience to] the old code of written regulations, but [*under obedience to the promptings*] of the Spirit in newness [of life]."

I like The Amplified Bible's wording even better because it makes an important point. You see, your flesh likes formulas. Your flesh wants to be told, "OK, here's the formula: If you pray three hours a day, you'll have an amazing life." For instance, a lot of times we read about people who did certain things or prayed a certain way and revival broke out. But we cannot adopt another person's pattern and expect it to work the same for us. If we do something because another person did it and got a certain result, then it becomes a formula to us. The life of the Spirit would not be in it because He prompted another individual to do it—not us.

Let me give you an example. David Brainerd, a man of great prayer who lived in Pennsylvania in the 18th century, used to enjoy praying in a tree log. Yes, that's right. The man climbed into a log and prayed for days and days until a revival broke out. Does that mean if you crawl into a tree log and pray for days and days like he did that a revival will break out in your town? God help you. You might rot in that log, and God will have to send Christians to revive you.

Again, The Amplified Bible says, "... so now we serve not under [obedience to] the old code of written regulations, *but [under obedience to the promptings] of the Spirit* in newness [of life]." Paul said we are no longer led by the law, but we are led by the *promptings of the Spirit of God.*

So what do we serve under now? We serve under obedience to the promptings, to the leading and the guiding of the Holy Spirit. That's our life now. Our life now is that we live and move and have our being in Him as Acts 17:28 says. So today we may come into a place where we receive from God and read the Word and pray all day long. But tomorrow if we cannot do that, we're still OK because God is still in us. God doesn't leave us or depart from us. God does not say, "See here, you're not praying enough."

No, that sounds a lot more like the devil to me. As I mentioned earlier, I've learned something about the devil, and you know what it is? If you pray six hours every day, the devil will jump on your case and say it's still not enough. "You're not praying enough. You should have prayed seven hours today. You need to pray more." But, Church, we live under the new covenant, and we already have God in us, our hope of glory. Now the only thing we need is to be ever aware that God is in us. We must establish our faith in Him to guide us by His promptings and His leadings and not how He guides and prompts someone else.

> WE MUST ESTABLISH OUR FAITH IN HIM TO GUIDE US BY HIS PROMPTINGS AND HIS LEADINGS AND NOT HOW HE GUIDES AND PROMPTS SOMEONE ELSE.

If you're a born again Christian, you have a union with God. He will give you His thoughts. He will move through you. He will move through your hands. He will move through any part of you that you will commit and dedicate unto Him. His promptings will move through you by the anointing and the unction of the Holy Spirit living inside of you.

So whatever you do—on your job or wherever you find yourself—do it unto God. Then you'll please the Father, and you'll be doing the right thing the right way. God may change your course along the way, but meanwhile you cannot be thinking your natural life is wasted or unnecessary or you desire to shed it off. You cannot do that! No, it's one life, one God, one you and one Holy Spirit—and thereby, you and I live our life in union with God.

'NO LONGER I WHO LIVE'

One of my favorite scriptures is where Paul wrote, "I have been crucified with Christ; *it is no longer I who live*, but Christ lives in me; and the life which I now live in the flesh I live by faith in the Son of God, who loved me and gave himself for me" (Galatians 2:20 NKJV). Paul was explaining that when Jesus died, Paul also died to himself. In other words, the "old" unborn again man had died when Paul received the work of salvation that Jesus accomplished at the crucifixion.

Notice one particular phrase from the verse again, "It is no longer I who live." That's how we also are called to walk. So wherever we go and whatever we do, we must do it unto the Lord and do it by the faith of the Son of God. Then in this way and from this position, we will begin to increase in Him.

When I realized that God called me to live one life instead of two, then I began to live my one whole life very differently. I began to enjoy my whole life, and I began to realize that my entire life needed to be acceptable to God and contribute to the will and plan of God in the earth. Therefore, the fellowship with the Holy Spirit and the enjoyment of the manifest presence of God that I had previously reserved for the spiritual side of my life needed to be incorporated into my entire life. The gateway of His presence was opened into my entire life and rippled and flowed even into the routine and mundane details of my life.

His presence changed my whole life; *His presence changes everything.*

Get a hold of this, Church. Everything flows out of our fellowship with God every single day—everything we do, everywhere we go. Our whole life becomes a continual fellowship with the Holy Spirit. Our whole life—our spiritual life, our home life, our relationships with loved ones, our job, our church life and even our ministry—are all one contribution to the plan of God

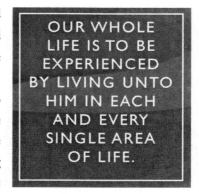

OUR WHOLE LIFE IS TO BE EXPERIENCED BY LIVING UNTO HIM IN EACH AND EVERY SINGLE AREA OF LIFE.

We must do all that we do unto the Lord for that is what He has called us to do. Our whole life is to be experienced by living unto Him in each and every single area of life.

He's calling us to take our place in this hour. He's calling us to demonstrate His glorious presence for all the world to see.

CHAPTER **10**

LIVING IN A TIME
OF OUTPOURING

I n these last days, we can and must be a people who walk with God every day all day long until we are no more. We're living in a time of outpouring, and because we are, we must understand the importance of walking with God always without exception. In fact, in the time of outpouring, if you don't continue going and growing and increasing in God every single day, you'll face some of hell's manifestations that you don't want in your life.

Church, this is the truth. I'm telling you this by the Spirit of God, so listen carefully to me. God means what He says. We're accountable for what we know; we're accountable to live by the power and the presence of God. We're accountable to stand in all that we've been taught; we're accountable to stand in the faith and the anointing that have been imparted to us.

No generation has had invested into them what we've had invested into us. We should be the most victorious people of any generation because of the teaching and the light we've received from God's Word. And we should be a people consumed with taking the gospel message around the corner and around the world so others may also know and walk with God, escaping the corruption that's in the world and yet to come.

Church, it's time to get the walk and the talk together.

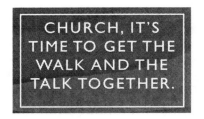

CHURCH, IT'S TIME TO GET THE WALK AND THE TALK TOGETHER.

Sure, we'll miss the mark from time to time. Who doesn't? Yet, because we keep ourselves in Him, we'll know when we err and we'll get right back into line because we live in union with our God. That's how Jesus lived; He lived in the union that He was in the Father and the Father was in Him. You also are in Him. You also are one with Him, and you do it by faith.

This union is the reason Jesus gave His life. Jesus' death, burial and resurrection were for the purpose of preserving the vital union between God and man. That's right. He hung on the cross, suffered untold pain and torment and surrendered His very life so our union could be restored. So can it be over-emphasized? It cannot. Paul said in Ephesians 6:10 "...be strong in the Lord [*be empowered through your union with Him*]; draw your strength from Him [that strength which His boundless might provides]."

Of course, your mind struggles to wrap itself around the leadings and promptings of the Holy Spirit. Your mind says, *What? Huh?* My mind says the same thing. But if we want to be spiritually alive and receptive to God and walk with Him day by day, then we'll have to increase our awareness of Him.

In fact, listen to this: *To the same degree you are receptive to the Holy Spirit all day, it's to that same degree you'll experience His manifestation that day.*

In like manner, the more we respond and cooperate with Him, the more we will increase in Him, and the more we will increase in revelation and experience. In effect, our response to Him increases our sensitivity to His voice. We grow in this experience of living in His presence, and it is by His grace and our faith in His leading us.

The Holy Spirit wants to take us some place, Church. He wants to take us deeper into the things of God. He wants to take us into the greatest time of our lives where manifest blessing is without measure. Yet, to walk in a new level of awareness and intimacy with God, we will probably need to make changes. Most of us will need to instill a greater discipline in our lives, and most of us need to decide to go forward differently than we've walked last year or in previous years.

Perhaps last year was even a good year for you, but still your heart is crying for more. I believe you want more. I know I want more. And God has more. God has spoken it by His prophets who have declared it, and He does nothing until He tells His prophets first. I believe with all my heart that God will manifest blessing in your life without measure, if you believe and cooperate with Him. That's why I'm sharing how you can cooperate with Him in practical ways, so you'll be skilled to follow where He's leading, guiding and calling you.

Let me encourage you to make yourself aware of God and His presence minute by minute. Begin to say from your heart, "Spirit of God, You are with me. You are in me." Then respond as He speaks to you and prompts you. Perhaps the Holy Spirit will lay the name of a person on your heart and prompt you to make mention of him or her in your prayers. If you obey the prompting, right there you will have increased because you obeyed and acted on what He spoke to your heart.

On the other hand, pray-ers will gladly tell you that not all Holy Spirit-led prayer is a quick mention. What if the Holy Spirit leads you to pray six hours on the floor? Quite honestly, He sometimes leads that way. I've enjoyed some marvelous prayer meetings of six hours on the floor in the spirit. Of course, you could never do that unless you were in the spirit, and you could never follow and obey Him without His grace. It's important to remember that everything the Spirit of God leads you to do, He graces you to do.

Still you might think, *No way, not me. I'm not doing any six-hour prayer meeting.* But, Church, when we get over in the spirit, we lose track of time; the Holy Spirit moves us out of time. The spirit realm is a timeless place. God created time for our lives on earth. But in these last days, we will learn to live outside of time if we plan to fully walk in the spirit.

Then again, the Holy Spirit may prompt you to call up or text someone simply to say, "I love you!" Perhaps He'll lead you to send a card. Perhaps He'll lead you to connect through an e-mail. I send out e-mails all the time by the leading of the Holy Spirit. I e-mail people just obeying promptings because I purpose to live under the promptings of the Holy Spirit.

Perhaps the Holy Spirit will lead us to "make mention" to God of a person or thing or event. Paul said, "I do not cease to give thanks for you, *making mention of you in my prayers*" (Ephesians 1:16). Making mention can surely be a Holy Spirit leading, and He leads me to make mention often. Most importantly, as I keep training myself in these ways, I keep experiencing the manifest presence of God. His manifest presence is a supply that strengthens my spirit and makes me strong and keeps me going on and on, further and deeper in God.

LIVING IN THE MANIFEST PRESENCE OF GOD IS A CHOICE.

Listen, Church, living in the manifest presence of God is a choice. It's a choice we must make in order to go forward in God. We must make the choice and then contend against the natural, physical sense realm, which will always try to crowd out God's presence in our lives. The natural way of life tries desperately to pull you and everything you do into the flesh to do without Him. It's Mary and Martha all over again.

A LESSON FROM MARY AND MARTHA

The story of Mary and Martha in Luke 10 is a prophetic word for the Church in these days. You recall that as Jesus was teaching in Martha's home, she busied herself preparing a meal for Jesus and other guests while Mary chose instead to focus on Jesus' teaching.

When you think about it, Martha's activity was very understandable. She was hurrying about to make things nice for Jesus. After all, Jesus was a guest in her home. Think about how you are about preparations when you have company coming, and then imagine Jesus coming for dinner at your house. But Mary sat at the feet of Jesus to receive His words, which is exactly what Martha needed to be doing at that moment.

We all know the place where cares try to take us over, get us all worked up and make us fretful. I'm learning this principle and working on it in my life, even though I've by no means perfected it yet. But the question we must continually ask is this: *What is the Holy Spirit saying to do at this moment?*

We simply cannot allow cares and duties to choke out the leading of His Spirit that is infinitely more needful in our lives. Like Jesus said to the woman consumed with cares and details, "Martha, Martha, you're so worried, and you're so anxious about so many things. Yet, Mary has chosen the *best thing*." Think about that. Mary chose the best thing. Are you choosing the best thing?

If we want the best, then we must choose the best. But listen, Church, choosing the best thing is not sitting at Jesus' feet all day long, nor is it sitting at Jesus' feet listening only to get up and walk off our own way. Choosing the best is sitting at the feet of Jesus, listening at His feet and then walking off together with Him.

We must walk together with the Spirit of God step by step following His promptings. Sitting at our desks, driving in our cars or doing whatever jobs we do, *we must practice His presence*. We must allow Him to move in us, prompt us and give us answers to problems right where we're working. In cultivating this receptivity to His promptings, we cultivate our relationship with Him. We increase in God.

WALK ON TOGETHER

Remember, your walk with God is just that—a walk. It's progressive, and it's a step-by-step cultivation of His presence. So if you miss a prompting today, don't give yourself a bad deal over it. Determine to do better tomorrow. If you missed His promptings all day today, say out loud, "Holy Spirit, I'll do better tomorrow! You are the grace in me, enabling me to grow in following Your presence."

The Holy Spirit is in this with you for the long haul. So trust Him to empower you to obey and follow His promptings, and down the path you'll most certainly reach the destination He has for you. Day by day by day by day—prompting by prompting—He'll go before you, leading the way, so the two of you can walk together.

Let me share this example. A while back my husband, Skip, and I had guests stay at our home for a couple of days and nights. As our guests prepared to leave, I stood in the driveway of our home telling them goodbye. Then as I walked back into the house, suddenly the prompting of the Holy Spirit hit me, "Pray! And pray right now!" So I began praying in other tongues while I was vacuuming, and I prayed and prayed in tongues for about 20 minutes.

When I finished, the Holy Spirit said, "Why don't you ask me what you were praying about? The Word says you can interpret your prayers."

That's a good idea, I thought, *I think I'll do just that.*

"Holy Spirit," I said, "What was I praying about?"

Just as quickly, the Holy Spirit manifested His presence and answered me. He told me things about our lives for that time period and for the future, and I haven't been the same from that day to this. I was hooked from that day on. I decided at that very moment that I would live in the manifest presence of God for the rest of my days. I hadn't always up until that time, but it became my purpose from that moment on.

I was captivated. I was enthralled. I realized there was no better way to live than to be intimately connected and communicating with the creator of the universe. Why would anyone want to live any other way?

Church, we need to pray in tongues more than we ever have before, and we need to believe Him for the interpretation for what we're praying. So what did I interpret from my prayers? I heard the Holy Spirit say about my husband, "Skip will lose his job today; he's going to be fired. But in two weeks they'll hire him back, and he'll get a promotion and a raise." Hallelujah! He provided me with inspired information about our lives. He showed me things present and things to come just like Jesus promised the Holy Spirit would do.

The Holy Spirit was manifesting—manifesting the present and the future—because that's who He is. Minutes later Skip called and gave me the news, but the Holy Spirit was already in front leading and guiding, and the answer was already there as well. That's how we can walk with God, and it's available to all of us who are born of God. That's how Jesus walked, and that's the grace you and I have in this time and this day.

KEEP WATCH ON YOURSELF

As we walk on with God living in this time of outpouring, we must remain diligent, strengthened in our spirits and intertwined with the Holy Spirit. We must keep watch on ourselves continually, ever aware of things that would hinder us.

The particulars are different for all of us, but for instance, I don't like to go to movies. There are some movies I enjoy, but most usually I don't. I'm protective of my fellowship with the Holy One and anything that could diminish that fellowship.

Now, this is not one of those cases where I'm about to give you a list of do's and don'ts. That's what religion does. Religion is full of rules and it bosses you around saying, "Do this! Don't do that!" But that's no way to live; it puts you back under the law. The Holy Spirit is never like that.

As I've developed my awareness of the Holy Spirit through the years, He has guided me through the specifics that helped me be more and more sensitive. If I'm watching or reading or listening to something and my spirit starts drawing back and wincing or going, "Ooo." I just move away from it. I will not allow anything to deter or negatively affect my fellowship with the Spirit of God.

Don't misunderstand me. I'm certainly not going to tell you what to move away from. That's between you and the Holy Spirit. It's His job to lead you in this area. But let me offer this definition of sin that the mother of church pioneer John Wesley once wrote to him:

"... Whatever weakens your reason, impairs the tenderness of your conscience, obscures your sense of God, or takes off your relish of spiritual things; in short, whatever increases the strength and authority of your body over your ... [spirit], that thing is sin to you, however innocent it may be in itself" (*Susanna Wesley letter, June 8, 1725*).

The Holy Spirit will guide and prompt you in the application of those words. In fact, notice how the Holy Spirit moved on John to teach us about these things. First John 3:19-22 says, "By this we shall come to know (perceive, recognize, and understand) that we are of the Truth, and can reassure (quiet, conciliate, and pacify) our hearts in His presence, Whenever our hearts in [tormenting] self-accusation make us feel guilty and condemn us. [For we are in God's hands.] For He is above and greater than our consciences (our hearts), and He knows (perceives and understands) everything [nothing is hidden from Him].

"And, beloved, if our consciences (our hearts) do not accuse us [if they do not make us feel guilty and condemn us], we have confidence (complete assurance and boldness) before God, And we receive from Him whatever we ask, because we [watchfully] obey His orders [observe His suggestions and injunctions, follow His plan for us] and [habitually] practice what is pleasing to Him."

In other words, our hearts can be assured in His presence and be confident in our oneness with the Holy One because God knows all. If the Holy Spirit brings something to our attention that is not pleasing to Him, we need to promptly fix it, adjust it or back away from it. If we change these small things as He directs, then as a result we are changed from glory to glory. And if He doesn't bring anything to our attention, then we can have confidence before Him that we are practicing what is pleasing to Him.

> IF THE HOLY SPIRIT BRINGS SOMETHING TO OUR ATTENTION THAT IS NOT PLEASING TO HIM, WE NEED TO PROMPTLY FIX IT, ADJUST IT OR BACK AWAY FROM IT.

Truly, the Bible instructs us all to "...lay aside every weight, and the sin which so easily ensnares us, and let us run with endurance the race that is set before us, looking unto Jesus, the author and finisher of our faith..." (Hebrews 12:1-2 NKJV).

The Amplified Bible sheds light on the grip these weights and sins can wield on us when it says "...let us strip off and throw aside every encumbrance (unnecessary weight) and that sin which so readily (deftly and cleverly) clings to and entangles us...."

So I encourage you to listen to your own spirit. When you sense your spirit talking to you, be quick and sensitive to obey. Strip off and throw aside weights and sins that try to cling to you, entangle you and ensnare you. Move away from distractions and things that would separate you from your union with Him. By doing so, you draw close to your Father, and you will go higher in Him.

Let me encourage you in these last days and in this time of outpouring to walk into more of His light and allow more of His presence to be manifested through you. Let Him change you to look more like our Master.

Press in!

I remember at our church one time, a father came up to me and said about his son who had been away from God, "My son and I are getting closer and closer every single day."

"That's good," I said.

Then I thought, *The father has always been there. What was wrong?* The answer was the son had drawn back from the father and barriers separated them. Likewise, fleshly behaviors and attitudes would *try to* separate us from our heavenly Father. But, glory to God, the love of God helps us and removes barriers.

The flesh will keep us disconnected from the love of God, disconnected from the anointing of God, disconnected from the goodness of God, disconnected from the blessing of God, disconnected from the prosperity of God and every other good thing God has for us. But the job of the Holy Spirit is to help us remove barriers from our path and our fellowship with Him. Sin is a barrier, and that's why God hates sin. God loves us, but He hates sin because it's a barrier that prevents us from being close and living in our oneness with Him.

A few weeks ago, I messed up big time, but the Holy Spirit said, "Just repent. We're still one." And if we're born again, we are one with the living God. We're one with Him even if we make mistakes. Actually, we all make mistakes, so the key is to ask for forgiveness so the barrier of sin is once again removed.

No matter what mistake you might make, God is still with you. He promised in Hebrews 13:5 that He would never leave you or forsake you. The Amplified Bible reads "...for He [God]

Himself has said, I will not in any way fail you nor give you up nor leave you without support. [I will] not, [I will] not, [I will] not in any degree leave you helpless nor forsake nor let [you] down (relax My hold on you)! [Assuredly not!]."

Acknowledge today that He is with you. Wherever you go today and whatever you do, acknowledge Him. As you do, you will become more aware of the presence of God, and He will manifest in whatever way you need Him to manifest. Develop the awareness that even when you mess up, He is with you.

It was so sweet of Him that day I messed up to say, "Just repent! We're still one!" In other words, just repent or turnaround and go away from it, and it will all be fine. Really, isn't that sweet? That's just like God; that's His personality. He says nothing can separate us from the love of God—  nothing! Notice that He gives us His Word on the matter in Romans 8:38-39 which says, "For I am persuaded beyond doubt (am sure) that neither death nor life, nor angels nor principalities, nor things impending and threatening nor things to come, nor powers, Nor height nor depth, nor anything else in all creation will be able to separate us from the love of God which is in Christ Jesus our Lord."

However, condemnation, guilt, religion, works, hurts, offenses and unforgiveness all try to build long, wide, high walls between you and God, so refuse to let them separate you and God. As we saw earlier in God's Word, "There is therefore now no condemnation to those who are in Christ Jesus, who do not walk according to the flesh, but according to the Spirit" (Romans 8:1 NKJV). The Holy Spirit takes you from glory to glory and

THE JOB OF THE HOLY SPIRIT IS TO HELP US REMOVE BARRIERS FROM OUR PATH AND OUR FELLOWSHIP WITH HIM.

faith to faith, and the more glory you step into, the more glory that will manifest through you.

So we must stop condemning, judging and criticizing each other—and ourselves—and instead we must be drinking from His river and walking in His presence. There's glory in *you*. There's a glory in you waiting to be dispensed to the world.

'AWAKE MY GLORY'

Dear friend, the psalmist David said, "Awake my glory!" (Psalm 57:8 NKJV). Do it now. Wake up to the glory in you. Awaken! Awaken! The Spirit of God is ever present working in you, so cultivate His wonderful presence like never before.

Believe.

Stretch.

Acknowledge.

Connect.

Access.

God's presence is all around us, and we can and must carry it, tap into it and connect with it all around us. Brother Hagin gave this example. He said the Lord told him there is enough of God's presence in every hospital room to heal the sick. If we would make ourselves aware of God in every hospital room, imagine how many people would be healed. Hospitals could be emptied out as it has been prophesied would happen in the outpouring of His Spirit in these days. We'll see it in the days to come—the very days in which you and I are living.

Brother Hagin went on to explain that even though the presence of God is in every hospital room, still you may feel demons and every sort of unspiritual thing when you walk into a given room. But Brother Hagin would say to begin immediately accessing the presence of God by saying, "God is here. God is here. The power of God is here to heal." Why? Because the more you talk about God, the more you access His power. You may feel nothing—most of the time you won't—but He's there just the same. Praise God! We simply believe and begin to access His presence by faith, and His power will manifest.

It's true even now. He's here because we've talked about Him. Whether you feel His presence or not, begin to connect with Him. Begin to say, "You are here right now with me and in me. I draw upon Your presence. I love you, dear Father. Take me to deeper places in You. Flood me with your presence and channel it to the world."

Arise! Shine! "...your light has come! And the glory of the Lord is risen upon you" (Isaiah 60:1 NKJV). So access God's glory in your life, and let's be about our Father's business. Let's be about our Father's presence, for His presence changes everything.

WELCOMING HIS PRESENCE INTO YOUR LIFE

If you desire to welcome God into your life and be filled and flooded with His presence as we've shared throughout the pages of this book, the first step is to receive Jesus Christ as your personal Savior. Jesus is the only way to the Father and the gateway to everything that awaits you in the realm of the spirit.

If you have not made a commitment to Jesus Christ, I invite you to pray this prayer aloud with me right now. It's the most important decision you'll ever make.

Dear Heavenly Father,

I come to You in the name of Jesus. Your Word says "...whoever calls on the name of the Lord shall be saved" (Acts 2:21 NKJV).

You also said in Your Word "...if you confess with your mouth the Lord Jesus and believe in your heart that God has raised Him from the dead, you will be saved..." (Romans 10:9 NKJV).

I believe in my heart that Jesus Christ is the Son of God. I believe He was raised from the dead for my salvation. Jesus, I call upon You to come into my heart right now. I thank You for the price You paid for me.

Your Word says, "For with the heart one believes to righteousness, and with the mouth confession is made to salvation" (Romans 10:10 NKJV).

I do believe with my heart, and I confess with my mouth that Jesus is now my Lord and my Savior. Thank You, Father, for saving me today and making me a new creation in Christ Jesus. I believe I'm now born again.

If you prayed this prayer today, please share your good news with us by calling (918) 307-1643 or e-mailing us at prayerdept@gloriouslightchurch.org.

ABOUT GLORIOUS LIGHT INTERNATIONAL CHURCH

Glorious Light International Church (GLIC) first opened its doors in August 2005 in Tulsa, Oklahoma, with a group of people passionate to experience more of God.

What began as a core group in a small meeting room at the Tulsa Historical Center has grown into a thriving congregation of diversity that meets at the church's present location at the corner of 71st and Sheridan in Tulsa.

GLIC is as diverse as its home city of Tulsa, and its members are all at different places in their relationship with the Lord. Yet, what makes GLIC a family is not just their diversity, but what they share in common. The people of GLIC are hungry to see God manifested in their lives and their church. They believe firmly that church is more than simply a social gathering or a place to visit every Sunday. Church is a calling, and the people of GLIC believe their calling is clear:

- Empower people to live by the biblical truths of faith, love, healing, prosperity and righteousness.
- Heal the hurting and the oppressed and restore prodigals back to their place in Christ Jesus.
- Equip believers for full-time ministry and the call of God on their lives.
- Lead believers to a deeper place in the Holy Spirit, led by His voice and operating in His power every day.
- Build an army of mature believers and pray-ers.

- Take believers from religion to reality and from hurt and brokenness to wholeness and maturity in Christ.
- Stand firm and wage a good warfare against the kingdom of darkness.
- Declare and display God's glory to Tulsa and the world.
- Carry God's love, His hope and His light to a hurting, hopeless and dying generation.

If you hunger for more of God—for living life to your full God-given potential—then Glorious Light might just be the place for you.

For more information about the church, visit www.gloriouslightchurch.org.

CPSIA information can be obtained at www.ICGtesting.com
Printed in the USA
LVOW130613190612

286758LV00002B/1/P